MORON CORPS

MORON CORPS:
A VIETNAM VETERAN'S CASE FOR ACTION

By John L. Ward

Assisted by Dr. William E. "Gene" Robertson

Strategic Book Publishing and Rights Co.

Strategic Book Publishing and Rights Co.
12620 FM 1960, Suite A4-507
Houston, TX 77065
www.sbpra.com

ISBN: 978-1-62212-207-3

Book Design by Julius Kiskis

20 19 18 17 16 15 14 13 12   1 2 3 4 5

DEDICATION

We dedicate this work to all US service men and women,
particularly those who have served in conflicts and wars.
We hope they will all be appropriately compensated
for their honorable service.

I also dedicate this to the memory of my parents,
Eddie and Frances Ward.

CONTENTS

ACKNOWLEDGMENTS

Many long hours went into writing this book. I want to thank all my family and friends, who encouraged me to continue during the times when I faltered.

I especially want to thank my long-time childhood friend, Dr. Elmer P. Martin, Co-founder, with his wife Joanne, of the nation's first Black History Wax Museum, The National Great Blacks in Wax Museum in Baltimore, Maryland.

INTRODUCTION

One can ask the question; why tell another story about the war in Vietnam? Haven't we heard this story told repeatedly? Isn't it something that we, as a nation, should put behind us? I believe fervently that the story of the Vietnam heroes needs to be retold frequently. I believe that each generation should hear it, not only for what we experienced in Vietnam, but because we are still suffering and dying now. Vietnam veterans came home to a cold reception, and for the most part, they still feel unwelcome and unwanted.

I came back from Vietnam as a very different man from the one who left to serve his country. I witnessed the Vietnam War intimately from the trenches, as a marine who had to kill and was trying desperately not to be killed. I was wounded physically, and mentally, and I suffered the ravaging effects of Agent Orange. I came back with a burning desire to tell the story of my Vietnam heroes.

This story is about my Vietnam War experiences and my struggles on behalf of Vietnam veterans and their families, and about all who are interested in their plight. I hope the reader can learn some basic strategies that will enable veterans to win full benefits for those who still suffering from neglect and abuse. I feel an obligation to share the knowledge of not only what we experienced during the war, but also of what has happened to so many of us after. I am also fully cognizant that many Vietnam veterans lack the mental capacity, physical strength, and the political knowledge to wage a fight on their own behalf. Many of the combat vets struggle from day to day with post-traumatic stress disorder, with complications from exposure to chemicals, with unemployment woes, imprisonment, isolation, living on the streets, lack the information, consciousness, organizational support, and they struggle to find the will to take on the powerful Veterans Administration and the Defense Department.

These government entities have neglected their obligations to administer the benefits for those serving their country. Therefore, through my personal experiences as a Vietnam veteran, I will serve as another witness and advocate, seeking fairness for those Vietnam veterans whose patriotism and heroism have been relegated to disgrace and doom.

It is my intention that this writing will shed light on the tragedies and circumstances faced by Vietnam veterans in their search for survival after combat and the madness of war. It is my objective to bring about a better understanding of: the effects of exposure to herbicides, the immoral tragedies of the draft, the ineffective veteran's Affirmative Action, post-traumatic stress disorder (PTSD), and the failure of the US Veterans Administration. The problems that we faced as veterans, and that we are still facing today will continue, unless we speak up and advocate for change.

Chapter 1

BEFORE THE WAR
IN A SMALL RIVER TOWN

I was born February 4, 1947 in Glasgow, Missouri to Francis and Eddie Ward. I was the youngest of eight children. My father worked on the railroad and my mother worked as a domestic. Both worked hard all their lives. They struggled and deprived themselves to provide for their children. I never heard them complain. We wore hand-me-down clothes and old shoes that were often either too big or too small. We often had to take a piece of cardboard with us to school, to make strips that covered the holes in our shoes. When the old strips got wet, we replaced them with dry ones to protect our feet. We lived in a shanty that required us to save old food cans to catch water when it rained, because our roof leaked. There were gaps in the walls where we could see outside without using the window, and in the winter, the snow swirled inside.

Winters were terrible, and we never ventured more than three feet from the old wood and coal-burning stove, to keep warm. Any venture to the kitchen or any other part of the house required full dress in winter clothes, because the rest of the house was as cold inside as it was outside. When we did go out, we wore unmatched socks for gloves, and old stocking caps, pulled down over our ears. We cut the wood with crosscut saws and axes, and used it to fuel the stove for cooking, heating, and washing. We carried water several blocks, because most black people in our community didn't have running water. We would pay a small fee to the few black families who were fortunate enough to have water faucets inside and spigots outside their homes.

Our existence was a step or two above that of a sharecropper; but somehow we managed. We scrubbed our clothes by hand with homemade lye soap and hung them outside to dry. In the winter, they would often freeze before they dried.

Food was whatever showed up. Wild game was the primary source of protein throughout the black neighborhood, and there were usually two or three rounds of ammo lying around. Our family truck was a homemade wheelbarrow. We put many miles on it bringing groceries home, hauling coal, wood, water, and chitterlings. The closest thing we had to a family doctor was my mother, who used old home remedies for everything and rather magically, or miraculously, her remedies would work.

For fun, the younger kids played at the city dump; sometimes retrieving the remnants of old toys. We then used these parts to make a variety of things, like sleds, homemade wagons, cowboy paraphernalia, and anything that we thought could be fun. Often, we took old tires home, filled them with dirt, rolled them away, and ran chasing them around the neighborhood, creating small dust storms. We played marbles, jacks, hopscotch, and hide and go seek. Many times, I would just go to the woods and look for snakes, swim in the muddy creeks, and then fish for catfish and "crawdads."

To help at home we often worked, household chores notwithstanding. Usually, it was working for local farmers. We would put up hay bales, pick potatoes, cut tobacco, shuck corn, or do other related, unskilled agricultural labor.

I, along with other youth of my era, started out in an all-black school. I actually loved it, even though I sometimes ran into trouble with the teachers, which were two black women and a black man. We respectfully called our teachers, "professors," because they were dedicated and showed us the utmost commitment to our education. They introduced us to a vision of life beyond cutting tobacco, and agricultural labor.

The all-black high school was centrally located in Dalton, Missouri, so it could serve the needs of black families in several small towns. They had excellent black teachers and administrators. By the time I entered high school, it was desegregated. The black students attended public schools in Glasgow, our elementary and high schools were closed.

Glasgow was located in Howard County, one of several counties known as, "Little Dixie." Originally, emigrants from Kentucky, Virginia, and Tennessee settled there. They brought slaves to the area in large numbers, which made Howard County the most predominate slave-holding region in the state of Missouri. Slave labor also made Howard County a prosperous area. With Glasgow situated on the river, it was even more prosperous than the other towns in the Little Dixie area.

Our parents, even with their own limited education, had always taught us that education was an important and necessary tool for advancement and success. It did not take much to see that white people in the Little Dixie area owned all the land, banks, stores, farms, and the good paying jobs. Many of the black students dropped out of school because they were tired of being treated with contempt and disdain. I decided to make my mark in music. I became recognized as one of the top trumpet and coronet players in the high school's history. The graduation rate in the all-black high school was considerably higher than that of the integrated high school. The most hopeful thing our "integrated" education gave us was the motivation to get out of that place as soon as we could. Most of us wanted to seek a life in a larger place, preferably in a large city, far away from Little Dixie. We constantly daydreamed about such a place□any place that offered better economic opportunities.

My father, Eddie Ward, was a hardworking railroad man, who killed himself to provide for eight children and a wife. He scrapped to stay in good standing with the local storeowners for food and heating fuel. There are photographs of him and his wheelbarrow, filled with chitterlings from the local meat locker. Eddie Ward instilled high standards through his stern behavior. We children respected and appreciated his example. He was not formally educated, but he was extremely wise.

My mother, Francis Ward, toiled relentlessly as a domestic. She would forgo her own needs to provide for her family. She had only two dresses and one pair of rundown shoes. She committed her life to her family. When my brother and I went into the military, we sent money home. She would not spend any of it. After she died, we learned about her saving the money for us. My memory of my parents centered on their sacrifices for their children.

When I was in high school, black people still could not sit in a white-owned restaurant and drink a soda or eat a hamburger. They had to go to the back door, the side alley, or some other place designated, "for colored only." During my parent's generation, racism was seldom confronted directly, or challenged openly. My father and mother believed that the way to defeat racism was through the long-term process of endurance, patience, and letting God work. They thought that by sacrificing then one day the younger black generation would know freedom. I thought that my generation was the one my parents had talked about, prayed over, longed for, and that I would soon know freedom.

I began by testing the validity of the civil rights law on my local level. My first endeavor came soon after the nation passed the Civil Rights bill. It was at a simple segregated pool hall. A few of my friends and I decided to go confront the owner of the establishment, to let him know that it was time for a change. As we entered, the owner was polite and accommodating. After all, he was accustomed to selling us sodas, candies, and cigarettes. I informed the owner that we had come to shoot pool, and after some odd facial expressions on his part, he assigned us to shoot pool on a table in the rear. We were ecstatic and commenced enjoying the game. After discovering that no one was using one of the better tables, we elected to try it out, since it was far more fitting for a good game. That was when he approached us sternly, "Now, you boys don't shoot on this table, you shoot on the table in the rear." I relayed to him that no one was using this table and that this is where we wanted to play. He thought about it for a minute and conceded that it was okay.

I felt elated. I felt as if part of a barrier had broken down and we had overturned a an unfair tradition. I could see myself as that generation in transition, from segregation to real, genuine freedom. I saw myself alongside thousands of marching feet, treading the path toward freedom, justice, and equality.In spite of these small social gains, Little Dixie offered few opportunities to rise beyond menial labor and poverty. Many of the young men could hardly wait until they were old enough to join the military. They did this not only to enjoy greater economic opportunity, but it was the chance to get outside the narrow confines of a small-town existence, and to see other parts of the world. It really didn't even seem to matter that a war was going on. In fact, we weren't even aware of the war yet.

In my case, I managed to stay in high school until my senior year. I intended to leave with a diploma in hand. During the very last day of my senior year, I had a problem with a racist teacher, which resulted in his flunking me. This left me one credit short of what I needed to carry away a diploma. In addition, I had scored below the minimum IQ standard on the military entrance test, and I had suffered a previous back injury. Without a diploma, these factors made me ineligible for enlistment into the Marine Corps. I began to think that my opportunity to use the military as my ticket out of Glasgow was doomed without a high school diploma. I knew that there was no chance in hell of getting the teacher to change his mind. Moreover, he was the only one teaching the course I needed to graduate. I had no choice but to explore other options. I could leave Glasgow for Kansas City or Des Moines, where many blacks in the community had already relocated.

Then the unexpected happened, the Army came knocking on my door. They led me to believe that I could simply go where they wanted me to go, and I would now be eligible for service, despite being ineligible before. Then, to my utter surprise, the Marine Corps recruiter showed up, and explained to me that I could join them now, even without the diploma, in spite of the previous back injury, and with a less than a desirable IQ score. I could now pursue my dream of getting out of Glasgow and seeing the world.

Thus, I was off to the Marine Corps, totally unaware, as were thousands of other disadvantaged blacks, Latinos, and poor whites across America, that President Lyndon B. Johnson, Defense Secretary Robert McNamara, and Daniel P Moynihan (advisor to the President) had made our stint in the military possible with Project 100,000.

Chapter 2

PROJECT 100,000:
THE DISCARDED ARMY

Project 100,000 was an idea concocted by the Johnson Administration to bring 100,000 poor youth into the military each year during the war; youth who had previously been termed, "rejects," for failing to meet the Army's mental aptitude standard. The program was sanctioned to train and salvage what Moynihan called, "...part of America's subterranean poor," by providing them with the training, skills, employment, and Veteran's benefits that they could use in civilian life to strengthen their families and communities. The truth of the matter was that the administration developed Project 100,000 to supply the desperately needed manpower to fight the war in Vietnam. The intent was to get the poorest, least educated, and most neglected American people to fight in the controversial war. The same war that the children of the, "best and the brightest," were protesting against, were getting special exemptions from, and who found ways to dodge the draft.

One general in Johnson's administration referred to Project 100,000 as the, "Moron Corps." Morons definitely were never expected to tell their stories, and the thousands who died in the war would never be able to. I am one of the recruits for whom the Department of Defense lowered its standard.

At the time, I was unaware that in a think tank atmosphere, these leaders had found a means of recruiting or drafting bodiescannon fodder to man their police action. The conflict was gaining momentum when the Gulf of Tonkin incident provided a justifiable political excuse to mount a war effort openly in Vietnam. Then the problem facing the Defense Department and the Johnson Administration was a lack of eligible fighting men to keep the communist North Vietnamese from toppling the fragile South Vietnamese regime. This regime had allied with the Americans against the North Vietnamese government, after the French had taken a major defeat, and had bailed out with heavy losses.

With the push to escalate the action, savvy parents with the financial means began to send their sons off to Canada, or into college in an effort to avoid the draft. These events led to the recruitment of the Project 100,000 men.

President Johnson and Defense Secretary Robert McNamara's proposal reduced the minimum standard IQ requirements for military recruitment, enabling the government to draft those who had previously scored in the lowest percentile on the IQ test. This allowed the military to draft some men who had barely missed passing the mental standard; they were also able to enlist some men who were dangerously close to the gray area, classified as mental retardation.

To add some appeal to the proposal, Johnson, McNamara, and Moynihan decided to write in special provisions that would provide special training, aside from the regular benefits by Title 38 of the United States Code (veterans' benefits). In other words, they created Project 100,000 under the guise of providing training in job skills to disadvantaged Americans. However, the special training these recruits received were in for occupations that did not require much education. The training focused on the use of common sense, and of course, the ability to follow orders. Out of the 15,000 professional skills that the US military offered, these recruits only received enough educational training to do menial tasks, and to carry a rifle these recruits were relegated to the lowest echelons of infantry.

Project 100,000 was no better at providing skills than any other government programs. It would not prepare impoverished young men with the skills for a better life in society. Instead, as one black journalist, Samuel F. Yette stated, it was, "Little more than an express vehicle to Vietnam."

Not only were Project 100,000 recruits made eligible under the reduced mental standard, but also large numbers were medically remedial cases (men with correctable physical problems). Many of these men were afflicted with chronic disorders such as cancers, tuberculosis, and a host of other diseases. Others came with severe problems of alcoholism and drug addiction. The administration promised them treatment for these ailments. The military leadership should never have inducted or accepted these men for military service, in any way. These men should have been profiled upon induction and sent back home. In my case, I had a serious back injury that was brushed aside as a birth defect. Many of these soldiers were unaware of the physical problems they had prior to induction.

However, when they returned home, after having served their country in a foreign land, with an aggravation of these pre-existing injuries or defects, the VA told them these medical problems were not "service connected." Then, if these veterans did not know their rights under Title 38 of the US Code, many were misinformed that there was nothing that could be done regarding those prior injuries. Some who were aware of the aggravation of their pre-existing injuries were denied any medical treatment. In many cases, this only allowed the Veterans Administration to avoid upholding their obligations to pay disability compensation. It was just another way to shortcut those veterans, now that they had outlived their usefulness.

The following information was later released by the Department of Defense regarding Project 100,000.

1Project 100,000: The Discarded Army

"Military Service," Moynihan wrote in his 1965 report on the Negro family, "is disruptive in some respects. For those comparatively few who are killed or wounded in combat, or otherwise, the personal sacrifice is inestimable. But, on balance, service in the Armed Forces over the past quarter century has worked greatly to the advantage of those involved. The training and experience of military duty is unique; the advantages that have generally followed in the form of GI Bill mortgage guarantees, federal life insurance, civil service preference, veterans' hospitals, and veterans' pension are singular, to say the least."

Increasing the number of blacks in the military was neither the first, nor the only measure Moynihan had advocated for those who were being rejected by the Armed Forces. Shortly before his death, President Kennedy established a Task Force on Manpower Conservation under Moynihan's direction, to study the one third of the male population who failed to qualify for the selective service. The task force found, not surprisingly, that the 600,000 individuals who were rejected annually were, to a large degree, the products of impoverished backgrounds and substandard schools. A disproportionate number were black.

---

1 THE DISCARDED ARMY: Veterans After Vietnam, Center for Study of Responsive Law

The Selective Service Rehabilitation Program (STEP) was developed. The idea was that people should be provided with services because they failed a test.

Legally, the military was free to accept anyone with a score above the tenth percentile. When manpower needs increased, the Pentagon could simply take more men with scores in the ten to thirty ranges (Called Mental Group IV) and use them for low aptitude assignments.

The new program would involve 40,000 men the first year, and 100,000 each year thereafter, hence the name Project 100,000. However, STEP would have lowered standards only for 11,000 volunteers. Project 100,000 would reduce standards for both volunteers and draftees. "The Poor of America," the Defense Secretary told an audience in New York City, "have not had the opportunity to earn their fair share of this nation's abundance, but they can be given an opportunity to return to civilian life with skills and aptitudes, which, for them and their families, will reverse the downward spiral of decay."

In less than two months, his department announced that it would reduce qualification standards after all, and admit the Project 100,000 men. The new inductees would be drawn from those who scored between the tenth and fifteenth percentiles on the qualification test.

Project 100,000 soldiers were not about to be assigned to training in the 15,000 professional skills that the US military offered. While the Defense Department had reduced the aptitude requirements for entering the military, there was no intention reduce requirements for technical positions within the services as well. These untrained and unqualified men were classified as the "New Standards Men."

We were drafting young black men who had been crippled by disparities in our society and sending them 8,000 miles away, to guarantee the liberties of people living in Southeast Asia, but these same men had not found the same liberties in South Georgia and East Harlem. The cruel irony was that we were repeatedly faced with images on TV of Negro boys and white boys, who killed and died together for our nation, but we were unable to seat them together in the same schools. We watched them in brutal solidarity, burning the huts of a poor village, but we realized that these young soldiers could never have lived on the same block in Detroit.

Project 100,000 men were never informed about who they were. The decision to keep their identity confidential probably did help the men's self-esteem, as McNamara contended. (However, many soldiers referred to the group using the pejorative term, the Moron Corps.)

That the Pentagon intended to use these men for the same menial work and service in the infantry as it had in the past was evident in a memorandum that Kelly sent to the services in March 1971. "The normal flow of Group IV will still enable the Department of Defense to use people with lower mental capacity in jobs that are suited to their talents." Translated into ordinary English, that meant combat, supply handling, and simple mechanical work.

They were the men who went into the army with the least education and the fewest skills. While in the army, they were the most likely to become casualties, and were the least able to acquire further education. Pentagon studies indicated that about ten percent of Project 100,000 men never finished their service, because they were killed, disabled, or released with bad discharges.

The engineers of this proposal, President Johnson, Secretary of Defense McNamara, and Assistant Secretary of Labor Moynihan, did everything they could to get Congress to accept this immoral proposal in order to provide troops, (cannon fodder) for the Vietnam War. This failed in Congress, mostly on the grounds of being morally questionable. It was Moynihan's opinion that the military was a better career choice for the Negro, even though military service was "disruptive in some respects."

The inductees who had medical or mental problems, and were deemed unacceptable for induction, were supposed to be referred for medical treatment in the civilian arena. This did not happen. There were cases of mental and physical illnesses, and a host of other health problems uncovered among the inductees. Yet, they were accepted into the armed forces, and were sent away to Vietnam, regardless of their ailments. This was to be a Salvage Program and that didn't work either. None of the proposed benefits for the people involved in Project 100,000 worked, but they kept this immoral and illegal game going, in order to put men at the frontline.

Former Secretary of Defense McNamara later admitted to the news media that there had been bungling mistakes made during the course of the Johnson administration. However, he never directly admitted to the mistakes or to his involvement in the morally shameful events surrounding the unauthorized way that he, Moynihan, and President Johnson went ahead with Project 100,000. The administration moved forward with the program, despite the protests of Congress and civil rights activists, especially Dr. Martin Luther King, without even considering any of the special benefits outlined in the original proposal. Going ahead with Project 100,000 showed how insensitive, morally unjust, and inhumane they truly were, despite protests.

Chapter 3

THE MORON CORPS

So, there I was poor, black, with a back injury, and one credit away from having a high school diploma. I was ready to be a proud Marine. Black men have fought bravely in all the major American wars, only to come back home and face racial discrimination and prejudice of the worst kind. Maybe this time, it would be different, I thought. After all, America was in a process of change.

The Project 100,000 recruits went into the various branches of the Armed Forces, but primarily they entered the Army and Marines. No one told us about our special status. A decision was made to keep our status confidential to boost our self-esteem, and to keep us from being stigmatized as an inferior brand of recruit. While some of us succeeded in basic training on a par with regular recruits, many of "The New Standards Men," as the administration dubbed us, had to be "recycled" through basic training. This meant that after failing, they had to take basic training over again. Many of our group suffered from drug and alcohol addiction, and there were severe disciplinary problems. It was not long before the military leadership recognized that many of the Project 100,000 men were different, despite efforts to hide our special status. Little did Project 100,000 recruits know that the higher-ranking officers had dubbed them with the nickname, the "Moron Corps." Oblivious to our official status, we were warriors. Even with our so-called limited abilities, we were willing to lay down our lives for our country.

Private Woods, for instance, was a Project 100,000 draftee from Texas. The first time I saw him was at boot camp, and he walked as though his feet were hurting. As time went on, our platoon mates and I were aware of the awkward gait of his every step, especially when he had to run. When we were on a ten-mile run, he could not carry on alone. Private Goldstone and I had to assist him by putting his arms over our shoulders and grabbing his belt on both sides; as we finished, we took him to the finish.

For this effort, I was given the position of squad-leader and was promoted to private first class. Private Woods also had problems with reading the basic training handbook. This was prevalent among many of the draftees. He was able to graduate from boot camp, and was sent off to the combat arena. I never knew how he fared during his tour of duty. Private Woods was black.

Private Gomez had some of the same problems, as well as an inability to stay in step with the cadence of the drill instructor. At one time, the drill instructor ordered me to kick his backside when he was out of step. When he did get out of step, I kicked him with some restraint, which caused the drill instructor to order the private behind me to kick my behind if I was light on Private Gomez. I didn't want any part of that, so I had to get tough with Gomez. I must say, I hated to do this, but it was him or me. The Platoon leadership sent Private Gomez to the motivational platoon (a disciplinary unit in the Marine Corps), and they set him back. This was a common occurrence. Private Gomez was Hispanic.

Many of these draftees had to contend with this same treatment. Some had the experience of having their finger smashed in the bolt of the M-14 for not releasing the bolt at the right time.

Later, at Khe Sanh, I ran into Chief. We called him that out of affection, not to besmirch him. He was very small in stature and thin. He looked terrible and carried an M-60 machine gun, which looked as though it was too heavy for him. His character was changed immensely, and it made me feel bad. This sight tore into my mind and has never left me, even until today. Chief was a Native American Indian.

I witnessed white veterans with a variety of ailments also. One of them was almost blind and could not see the target to test at the rifle range. This particular blind draftee was white. But most of these draftees with poor vision were black, more so than the rest of their population.

I embraced the term "Morons," but not because it was accurate. Many of us served our country too well. Many of us continued to have distinguished careers in the Armed Forces, long after the war was over. I became a Squad Leader, received good conduct medals, a Presidential unit citation, Vietnam combat medals, and other awards. I accept the term "Moron" to highlight that this is still the way the American social order sees and treats Vietnam heroes today. I keep the term to remind America that these "Morons" died in disproportionate numbers, thinking they were keeping democracy alive and promoting their country's interests. Those of us who managed to survive the war were literally thrown back into society, without the skills promised to us. This group of veterans has been imprisoned thirty-five percent more than the national average. One out of every five is homeless. Many suffer from isolation, unemployment, drug addiction, and medical neglect.

Our nation, which we fought for, has expected us to suffer and die in silence. More than 100,000 Vietnam Veterans from all categories; whether the Moron Corps or regular Marine Corps have committed suicide since the war. So those of us so-called Morons who are able to, must speak clearly on behalf of veterans who cannot speak. We must help them gain the basic tools to fight the system, to win the war that continues to rage within, and to never let anyone dubbed them morons again.

This was the battle I became caught up in, and consumed by. This was a battle that I fought over, and over again, continuing long after the Vietnam War was over.

Chapter 4

THE VIETNAM WAR

"**K**ILL, KILL, KILL," was the rallying cry throughout our Marine Corps training. Of course, nothing in my upbringing came close to preparing me to witness killing and death at this dimension and magnitude. We occasionally watched reenactments of the glories of World War I or World War II on television or at the movies. We clearly saw that the heroes who died in those movies appeared alive and well in the next. Compared to what was to come, my childhood and early adolescence seemed so unreal and innocent. It seemed so out of place that a small town boy would find himself in full fighting gear on a plane, headed for the unknown, where so many other small town boys never returned home alive.

For the first two years of service, I served stateside, trained in Supply Administration, and was a member of the Marine Corps Band, but eventually I was on a plane to Vietnam.

On that plane, there was apprehension on the faces of some, but still, plenty of others were boisterously gung-ho. "I'm-gonna-kill-all-the-Gooks-when-I-get-there," talk was rampant, a product of our training. Honestly, I was a bit on edge and somewhat in awe of our imminent arrival to the combat area. As the plane approached the landing at Da Nang, I stayed at the window, looking at the ominously dark jungle below. I wondered if I would see the flash of explosions, guns firing, or even the enemy trying to shoot our plane down. The closer we came to land, the more reserved and concerned everyone became, and the conversation on the plane quieted down.

All of the training, the gung ho talk, and the psychology of "kill, kill, kill," had left us with perceived notions of what it would be like when our turn came. Everyone became consumed with different impressions of what awaited us on the ground. The thought that it was all about to happen left a big lump in my throat, as I began to wonder if I would come out of this alive.

Upon arrival in Vietnam, we first faced the traumatic adjustment to the smell, the people, and the strange environment. Landing craft quickly took my battalion out to the awaiting ships, (the USS Okinawa, USS Iwo Jima, USS Fort Marion, and the USS Kearsarge). We were assigned afloat as a strike force, to be flown in by helicopter to the hot spots up and down the coast as reinforcements to troubled units inland. We also used the inland rivers to relieve troubled units. Here was when I first noticed combat Marines who appeared unable to adapt to stress the way the majority of the others did. No mistake, there was fear. The consensus was to adapt and overcome the pervasively harsh environment.

It was a place where one could never be comfortable. Moving from a float to the assigned areas inland brought about a rude awakening, because then we really had to bear with the environment. The mosquitoes seemed to attack in swarms, with multiple bites occurring simultaneously. All those Marines without mosquito nets immediately went to work trying to hustle one up, in any way possible. Even with a net, the mosquitoes seemed to find a way in. I recall that as a horrible experience, which made for long and highly stressful nights.

It didn't take long for the in-coming artillery rockets and mortars to join in and exacerbate an already worsening circumstance. Not much time had gone by, and most of us that were scattered to different units had already begun to experience the horrible sights of WIA's (wounded in action) and KIA's (killed in action). The first experience of seeing people killed and wounded in combat has to be one of the worst mentally traumatic sights witnessed by young green combatants.

I had to start my tour of duty in 'Nam attached to the 1st Battalion, 3rd Marine Regiment, and 3rd Marine Division. As Christmas got closer, I transferred to 1st Battalion, 12th Marines, and was pushed even closer to the Demilitarized Zone. Alfa 1/12 was an undermanned 105-mm howitzer artillery battery, based at Dong Ha. I received my experience with artillery big guns; loading, shooting, and passing ammo while in Dong Ha. Then quite suddenly, the battery was ordered to move even farther north, to Camp Carroll. Little did I know all that lay ahead for me.

In the process of moving, the outfit needed one more truck driver, and I was volunteered to convoy the six-by with trailer up the road a route filled with treacherous dangers. I didn't know what to expect, because I didn't know where I was going, nor had I the experience of driving in a convoy. As we prepared to get underway, I was told to stay close and, "We'll see you there." The experienced drivers were all in front and new drivers like me were in the rear. I was in last place. This was a lonesome spot, considering that I couldn't see the vehicles ahead because of the heavy dust, and I was afraid to stay too close for fear of hitting something in front of me, or of running off the road. So, I dropped back. When I could see through the dust, everyone was out of sight, and boy, was I alone? As I drove through the village of Cam-Lo with all the people standing beside the road trying to peddle wares, all I could think about was what if the Viet-Cong were among them, waiting to ambush the last vehicle?

The further I fell back, the more worried I got. I began to think I would probably miss a turn and all sorts of terrible things could happen. As I got further up the road, I saw the truck in front of me waiting at the turning place and I was overwhelmed with relief.

I spent Christmas at Camp Carroll in a stressful environment, which was supposedly truce time for the Christmas season. However, we were in the trenches with all the big guns leveled in preparation for a heavy ground assault that never came. I think that because of a full moon, the North Vietnamese army and the Viet-Cong decided it was too light to rush our position.

Everyone was elated when Big Red (the Sun) came over the horizon, even without sleep. Sleep was a rare comfort at Camp Carroll. For us, it was unheard of. With the big 175-mm guns with its 18-foot barrel blasting, the dust got very dense all around the immediate vicinity, making for one restless evening after another.

The New Year rolled around and things seemed to be quiet. Then, in the middle of the night, we were informed that some of us would be leaving at dawn the following morning, to serve as reinforcements for the firebase at Khe Sanh.

When I arrived, the Khe Sanh Valley was the most beautiful place I had seen in the jungle. When we disembarked from the choppers, it seemed to be wonderfully calm, and we were able to stay for a few days. I was assigned to Whiskey 1/13 (1st Battalion 13th Marine). This outfit was a 4/2 (four deuce) mortar battery with a refreshing Commanding Officer and Executive Officer. Even the troops were cool, so I felt good about the transfer. That was, until the First Sergeant jumped on me for no reason other than his own purposes. He was blatant with his discrimination and left no room for doubt.

One of the battery clerks who bunked with me, and was a friend, would often inform me of the First Sergeant's racial slurs and his plan not to promote me. It was my first encounter with open racism in 'Nam. All of my animosities toward the North Vietnamese Army and Viet-Cong seemed to gravitate to him and this took a lot out of me. Nobody else of any color had shown me that extremely distasteful and evil thing since being there. I was devastated by this. It was hard to imagine that someone who had to duck rockets, artillery, mortars, and bullets could find enough time to be a racist. Prior to that time, I was too busy being afraid to pay much attention to skin color. Now that I had become aware of him, I watched him closely.

Our alert status was upgraded, and now we had to wear our flak jackets and helmets at all times, in case of expected incoming rockets and artillery. There was no more eating hot chow in the mess tent. This place, which had seemed so serene and quiet, now took a turn for the worst. Those of us on the lower echelon, we were not privy to what was about to happen next.

On January 21, 1968, at 6:00 a.m., the Khe Sanh firebase began taking incoming fire from rockets, artillery, and mortars. That first onslaught of incoming fire created big fear and really woke us up. The first rounds were direct hits on the ammo dump. This set off numerous explosions, which blew other explosives out of the ammo dump and dropped them onto positions around it. Worse than that, the incoming rounds caused the rupture of our gas rounds. The gas then spread over the entire base and meant we had to wear gas masks. The temperature there during the daylight hours was extremely hot, and adding the gas mask made breathing more difficult. When the gas mask order was given, we didn't know if it was gas from the North Vietnamese or from us. It really didn't matter, because it still had the same physical effects. Some of the masks were screwed up, thus making a few soldiers very sick. Those who got sick were lucky, because it was only tear gas.

On the trench line, my assistant gunner and I operated one of many M-60 machine guns. This was a very tense position, because it was common knowledge that the fully automatic weapons (machine guns) were high priority targets from the enemy. Machine gun sites draw concentrated attacks, generally with rocket-propelled grenades (RPG's), which can wipe out a sandbagged position. As the day went on and the gas abated, we received harassing incoming rockets and artillery fire. This strategy was supposed to cause fear and destroy morale. I'll have you know that judging from the look on every face, the strategy worked. It didn't take very long to say to myself, "What the hell am I doing in the camp? What did I do to deserve this? I must indeed be a moron to end up in this hell hole."

That first night was sleepless, to say the least. We were kept on alert and everyone expected the enemy to make a big attempt to over-run our position. A very high state of tension prevailed all through the night. Right away, everyone on the entire firebase began to live underground; we prayed that our bunkers wouldn't take a direct hit. We soon witnessed direct hits on bunkers and saw the hideous death that this could inflict. The horrors were so very real, and yet it seemed like an unreal never-ending nightmare.

Those of us who had been in the bush for a while knew about brief ambushes and firefights. That style of conflict had been the norm. This on-going artillery barrage was new and awesome in its effects. The sound of an in-coming artillery round, about to land on or near your position was so frightening, that some Marines just lost it. The ominous language of those big devastating rounds falling out of the sky tested the mental limits of everyone so much so that I was sure we wouldn't be able to cope with another day of that madness.

My ears became conditioned to the sounds of guns firing from miles away, signaling the time to break for the nearest hole I could use for refuge. I often had scrapes and bruises from running and diving into holes, sometimes other people would dive on top and squeeze in. I never saw anyone put out or denied entry to an already crowded hole.

On the second day, the troops stopped using the outdoor toilets, especially at night for fear of being caught there during incoming fire. I witnessed an incident where a warrant officer was using the "head" adjacent to our bunker, and an incoming round hit it. They said that he lost his family jewels. No one thought this was necessarily funny; it was just how we talked. Today, this incident still has a tremendous emotional effect on me. That second day also ended our dining in the mess hall. The mess hall was a big tent with rickety benches and tables. It felt to me like being in the big city, and I wasn't accustomed to having it so good, hot chow and all. Now, it was not only the end to the good chow, it meant we were reduced to field rations, and there was a limited supply at that. The planes that resupplied us were either being shot down, blown up on the landing strip, or just didn't trying to land.

The North Vietnamese artillery had zeroed in on our landing strip where we waited for a plane to land. This resulted in the plane flying over and dropping supplies by parachute. That didn't prove to work so well, because the wind would take the chutes and goodies outside our perimeter, and we dared not go out to get it.

We had to endure water and food rationing due to the difficulty in resupplying. We always had to be ready to run for cover. Even if caught in the open, we had to hit the deck and get as far into that helmet as possible. Anything was better than nothing; one or two sandbags were shelter if nothing else was in close proximity.

There were times when C-130 planes would do the touch and go landings. This way they could come in high, dive for the runway and as soon as the plane touched down, the crew would release a parachute, which in turn, would pull the supply bundles out of the rear of the plane, allowing the C-130 to continue back into the air without a stop. That method worked okay but we wondered how to get drinking water. This was in the days before readily available plastic bottles of water. They couldn't do the water supply drop in the same way as the food drops. Eventually, the big choppers would fly in, hover over the base, and unhook the water buffaloes, which were mobile water tanks.

Through binoculars, I often watched air strikes involving F-4 Phantom jets, A-6 jets, and Cobra helicopter gunships, and I cheered with every explosion. It was the greatest relief to see and to know they were on the job. I witnessed one Phantom get hit, but I still didn't want to believe it. As I watched in awe, the jet arose from below the trees, and I saw something fall off the plane. I only realized that it was the pilot when I noticed the parachute open. My heart went out to the guy, because he was smack in the middle of the North Vietnamese troops. Everyone watching this event felt as though he could never make it. This pilot had just strafed and bombed these people. Immediately after he bailed out, other fighters and helicopters gunships hurried to cover him. They dropped everything they had, trying to make a safer passage for him. It worked, and oh boy, we were all glad that they plucked him from the middle of that madness. I continued watching the operation until I saw him climb out of the helicopter at the landing strip of Khe Sanh. I found out then that he was a major, and had hurt his ankle when he landed in the bush.

I felt that these horrible things couldn't really be happening, and I wondered what I was doing there. As the days and nights went on, the bombardment of mortars, rockets, and artillery continued incessantly. There were instances where some Marines were afraid to leave the bunker to make a bowel movement. They were then ordered to stop relieving themselves in empty c-ration (field ration) boxes, and tossing them out later. They had to hold it until the right moment, and then make a break for outside.

In our area, we surely would do anything to avoid using the assigned outhouse, since there was an unexploded artillery round buried in the ground directly beneath it. This was enough to dissuade anyone from using that outhouse. Our only alternative was to dig a quick cat hole (a six inch by one foot hole in the ground, to be used by one man, one time only), hurry to do our business, and beat feet back to the bunker. What happened to the warrant officer further enforced this. That was not something easy to put out of your mind. I saw guys doing it on the run.

Day in and day out, we faced this madness with the thought that we surely wouldn't make it out in one piece. if at all.

It wasn't long after the onset of the siege that President Johnson stopped the bombings. Among the guys around me, we all thought that he had to be crazy, or else, he didn't give a damn about our plight. We weren't the slightest bit interested in politics, we just needed help to get out of there.

At this point, it seemed that the enemy stepped up their artillery and everything else. What a discouraging feeling. The word came down that help was on the way, but many of us were certain that it was too far away. Water and food rations were short; we weren't sure whether our ammo would take us through this mess. The next bitter news reached us by way of the Stars and Stripes military newspaper. It said, "The besieged bastion on Khe Sanh, surrounded by an estimated two divisions (40,000) of North Vietnamese Regular Army Forces is being hailed as the walking dead." It wasn't good that we saw this; it was hard on our morale.

Some Marines were losing it. After all, we couldn't see much of anything positive that was happening. I find it difficult to express how I felt at that time, other than to say, "It's a terrible thing."

A black gunnery sergeant, whom everyone called Gunny, was considered to be half-crazy; he would stand around as if nothing was happening, while we all ran from incoming artillery shells. He would often try to convince me to join him, but to no avail. I would quickly retreat to my bunker with everyone else. We all discussed how crazy he was. He had previously served in Korea. Another sergeant, who was white, stayed in my bunker. He had serious problems with in-coming artillery. I witnessed his mental collapse. We were all worried about his stability. We were concerned that he would refuse to leave the bunker. In addition, he was armed so we worried that he was a danger to himself, or to anyone going in after him. He refused to leave the bunker to use the toilet. Eventually, he was later evacuated. He had also been a veteran of the Korean conflict. My gunnery sergeant assigned me to take care of one Marine, Private Lee. Lee was put in my care shortly after his mental breakdown. I tried to explain to the sergeant that my hands were full with other duties, and they would conflict with my watching Lee, but he was adamant. I followed his orders, and began to help Pvt. Lee the best I could. I told him that I was more afraid than he was, and that there was little time for talking. He was to do as I did, and we would both hoped we got it right.

Soon after that, Lee was like my shadow. When I ran, Lee ran. When I dove for cover, Lee dove for cover. He would dive right on top of me, too. I was constantly getting hurt because Lee was a large man, and caused a lot of damage. He was under such duress that he refused to speak, and they had to disarm him for fear that he would hurt himself or others.

Day in and day out, Lee and I would face incoming artillery, along with the challenge of just staying safe. In some ways, looking out for Lee was a very serious concern for me, because I had no idea how to take care of us both. I was pretty close to insanity myself. However, I do think that my having these heartfelt concerns for Lee helped me as much as it helped him.

Lee and I continued our daily runs for a few weeks. We would play checkers in the bunker together, and he even began to talk to me in a limited way. Soon after he began to open up, they medically evacuated Lee off the base, and I never saw him again.

Private Lee was not the only one who lost it on the base. There was also a staff sergeant, who was not allowed to defecate in his bunker. He completely broke down and had to be evacuated, too.

It appeared that if there was a God, he had bad things in store for us. Every day was long, and filled with the same horrors as the day before, and every night carried the fear that "this-is-it." As we manned the trenches, awaiting the onslaught of the suicide attackers, we watched the explosions of rockets and artillery all around us.

At some point, a few of us stood in a gun pit, preparing to fire, when a mortar round came in. It exploded two feet from my bunker, and the gun pit was about twenty feet from the blast. We immediately hit the deck. As I took cover, I heard the Marine who had been standing right next to me scream, "I'm hit." When I looked up, I saw that he had taken a chunk of shrapnel in the back. His next remark was, "All right, I'm out of here." He was out of there, but two weeks later, they sent him back and he was tremendously depressed. He got back just in time to receive the latest news. "They've got tanks moving on us."

By this time into the siege, the Marines at Khe Sanh had been without baths or showers for over a month, and had to wear filthy dirty clothes. There were huge rats sharing our bunkers, as if they also were afraid to go outside. With all of these bad things going on around us, it became quite difficult to be optimistic about our survival. I felt so lost, and at the same time filled with despair.

It seemed as though I had witnessed more horror than my tolerance could take. Every day and night was a struggle just to keep moving. What it was that kept me going, I've yet to figure out. Long into the siege, there finally came something good. President Johnson ordered the resumption of the bombing raids.

During the B-52 bomber raids, we were ordered to stay in the bunkers and trenches, due to the bombs being dropped just outside the base. Of course, many of us stuck our heads up to see the onslaught what a remarkable sight. The heavy bombs roared out of the sky, sounding as though they were coming down right on top of us. It had a chilling effect that is difficult for me to describe.

Anyone hearing this sound would instantly know that something was about to happen, something that had to be devastating beyond anything imagined. When these bombs started to explode, the ground shook and trembled violently, with dust in the air so thick I could hardly breathe. The bombs cut wide paths through the surrounding valley, uprooting whole trees and leaving holes in the ground, large and deep enough to drop a truck in. They fell, not one at a time, but exploded with the rapidity of machine gun fire. These drops would last for what seemed like fifteen minutes. I know that anyone out there had hell to pay. Oh boy, what a relief! We all shouted out our approval and thankfulness with a gasp of relief. To say that our morale was boosted would be an understatement. This bombing didn't stop the big guns from firing on us, but it slowed the frequency as the pilots poured it on.

Not long after the bombing began, the C-130 planes and helicopters began to land on the airstrip, bringing the goodies, food, water, and ammo. The bombs had been effective enough that they allowed the Army's 101st Calvary to break through to us, along with other support. At the end of the siege after seventy-seven days, we were ordered to abandon firebase Khe Sanh. Even then, I was afraid of the ride out of the valley with the convoy.

I quickly perched myself in a .50-caliber machine gun mount on the truck. I was seeking the reassurance of having control of that monster gun in the event of an ambush, which I'm glad to say didn't happen.

The convoy brought us to Quang Tri, which was quiet at that time deceivingly so where we were supposed to recuperate from our frightening ordeal. We all tried to settle down while we had the opportunity, but for me this wasn't enough. It was some relief, but in retrospect, it just didn't work. I took it upon myself to seek medical help, since I felt some kind of pressure that I didn't understand. The corpsman (medic) sent me to Da Nang for a psychiatric examination. They found that I had been under too much stress, so they returned me to my outfit, since they considered it to be in the rear, and supposedly this would allow the tension to settle. To some degree, this helped.

We soon moved to a new location along Highway One, called Phu Loc. This place was on a small hill, in the shadow of a much larger one. This was supposedly a generally quiet area, located close to our Battalion Headquarters. We spent a couple of weeks in relative calm, only dealing with mosquitoes. While dealing with the mosquitoes, I also had to deal with the first sergeant as well. Something had to give. In my mind, I felt that the right thing to do was to get myself away from him. After filing a complaint and a request to transfer, the word came down that a platoon of sappers (a Vietnamese suicide squad) was in the area. This information dominated my mind, while I worked on making my sleeping area more secure, bearing in mind that my rotation date to leave was getting near. I submitted a request to the gunnery sergeant to allow me to rig a large booby-trap near my bunker, which I felt was located in one of the enemy approaches. He thought I was being overly sensitive, because I was a short-timer, so he denied me access to the explosives I needed to set a trap. Guess what happened? At 3 a.m., on Sunday morning, August 17, a huge barrage of mortar fire hit us. I knew from this barrage that we would have soon be overrun with ground troops coming, because the Vietnamese didn't spend that much money on harassment. I was correct. Not long after the start of mortars, along came the ground assault, right under their own mortar fire.

My objective at this point was to get away from my bunker, since it was so close to the outer perimeter and make it to a gun pit further away from the perimeter. This would give me more of a chance to fight. As I made my move to do so, an explosion immediately to the right side of me hit me with shrapnel. The explosion blew me into the air for what seemed to be a few minutes. It felt as though I was stuck on a ceiling until I hit the ground, trembling with shock. I could feel one finger on my right hand flopping around as my body shook involuntarily. I don't know how long the shaking went on, but it finally subsided.

There was no pain, however. I knew that I had been hurt, but I didn't have a real idea of how badly. In my state of confusion, shock, and fear, my mind began to function enough for me to notice the loud ringing in my ears, along with what sounded like explosions and AK-47s firing. It also seemed as though none of our weapons were firing. My first reaction was to find my weapon, and I was trying to do this by feeling around on the ground. I looked up with blurred eyes, and in the flash of another explosion, I saw a Vietnamese soldier about thirty yards from where I was kneeling on the ground. As it happened, he saw me, too. In that second, he started firing and I started ducking. I could feel things hitting me, and hitting the ground under my body. I guess thought I was already dead, because for some reason I couldn't move. It seemed to me that I could feel the vibrations of feet running very near me. I also heard the Vietnamese shouting what seemed like orders.

As my thought processes started to come around, I began to fear that they would bayonet me. We knew this to be their custom under the circumstances. When that didn't happen, I gathered myself the best I could, and crawled behind some sandbags. I laid there and listened to the one-sided battle.

Chapter 5

BEING WOUNDED

.

The assault seemed to last forever, even though I knew different. Because in my experience with ambushes and firefights, they were violent and short events, yet devastating for the wounded and dead. As I lay behind the sandbags, I that felt the enemy would keep the hill and go around to make sure everyone was dead. I had no way of knowing how badly we were over-run. All of the horrors of the war now passed through my mind. I didn't know what was going to happen next, or if I would lay there and bleed to death.

I have never felt such a lonely and frightening moment. My fears went even higher when I saw flashes of light around the sandbags. I just knew that this was it. In my mind, all I could imagine was that the Vietnamese were making their rounds to finish me off. I was hoping that they would not find me. I tried to slow down my heartbeat, which seemed loud enough that anyone could hear from far away.

Then I heard men talking in English. It took everything I had left to make a decision whether to keep my head down and risk being left there or to take a chance of being shot and raise my head. I chose to raise my head. The light hit me in the face and the Marines asked me where I was hit. What a relief. I answered the best I could, that I was hurt all over. Then they asked me if I could walk. I answered that I would try. With this, I got to my feet, but immediately I felt myself starting to pass out and fall. Both Marines grabbed me before I hit the ground, placed me on an outspread poncho, and carried me to the lighted area where they were assembling the wounded and the dead. I remember seeing bodies around me that didn't appear to be breathing. Meanwhile, around the outside perimeter, a plane also known as Puff, the Magic Dragon sprayed major machine gun fire all over the mountain.

Soon after, they placed me in the assembly area. The corpsmen began to bandage me up as they found my wounds. This is when the awful pain struck. I was coming out of shock and felt overcome with intense pain from head to toe. I began to beg for a shot of morphine, but the corpsman refused, because it is standard procedure not to administer morphine for head wounds.

After some of the other wounded and I were loaded onto the truck, we were bounced around, and jostled unmercifully. This truck was taking us to the landing zone, but it had to stop repeatedly and slow down because of the screaming from the wounded. I woke up in a field hospital during transit in Phubai, which was where they started treatment for my injuries. I awoke with a chaplain and nuns standing over me, holding my hand. I did not think I was going to make it and neither did they. A nurse showed up with a needle and gave me something for the pain, which immediately put me out again.

None of what happened after I was injured was very clear to me until a few days later, when my mind began to organize my surroundings. It seems like during so much of that time, as things were happening to me, there were clouds and fog in my mind. I still wonder sometimes about it; it seems so unreal. A Marine who had fallen from a chopper and broken his arm approached my bed and said, "We didn't think you were going to make it, brother." After his remark, things started to look somewhat brighter. He went on to tell me that we were in Yokosuka, Japan, in a Naval hospital and he told me everything he had witnessed regarding my previous days there.

Now that I was conscious, they came again to change my bandages. I didn't want them to touch me anywhere, since I lay strung out in traction and all tied up. I pleaded with the nurses to wait a few days and then change the bandages, but my begging didn't work. There it was again, the horrible pain. I dreaded every day, because I knew that the bandage raiders were coming. There were others around me who screamed in pain as well, but it didn't give me any solace to know that. Let me tell you this, they never missed a day! The only good part was the nightly shot of painkillers.

I was told that for a short time, they had lost me and brought me back. I didn't know how to take this, but it did feel good just to be alive. Since I knew nothing about it, it didn't seem to matter much. I just wanted to go back to the world. It took forever for them to get me on a plane and out of there, but when the time came, it was a wonderful day. Riding in the big C-141 Air Force jet, was for me, a great thing. I was on my way back to the things I held dearest in my heart. Little did I know what I was about to endure during my thirteen-hour flight back to the states.

Once in the air, I had intense pain and airsickness. I began to grit my teeth, cry, and beg for painkillers. I did this for the thirteen hours until the plane landed. I was elated to be home. This was the first time I felt like I had a chance to survive. As soon as I had the opportunity, my first act was to call my dear mother, to whom I had lied the entire time I was in Vietnam. I had simply told her in every letter that everything was quiet and peaceful, I focused on describing the things in the jungle and villages, and avoided mentioning anything violent. Before I went there, I made sure that she would not be notified if I was hurt.

The Marine Corps had notified my eldest sister that I'd been wounded, but was alive. She made the decision to go ahead and tell my mother. I had no idea that my mother knew, and after I arrived stateside, I called her and continued to tell her that everything was fine. She never let on that she knew anything.

The military medical corps began to transfer me from hospital to hospital for treatment, tests, and recuperation. In a short period, I went from Travis AFB to San Antonio AFB, to Corpus Christy Naval Air Station, and then on, to Camp Pendleton.

Chapter 6

MY INJURIES

Being wounded by bullets, shrapnel, booby traps or bombs were not the only wounds Vietnam veterans suffered. We all came back with physical and mental wounds, beyond those that might have earned us a Purple Heart. There were the wounds we that knew about, and other wounds which we had no idea existed, because they were problems the government chose to camouflage. We all faced our wounds and disabilities, including PTSD (post-traumatic stress disorder), drug addiction, alcoholism, exposure to Agent Orange, and other toxic herbicides, and the many other medical problems that were connected to our experiences in Vietnam. Once we were home, our government determined that all of us, despite our wounds, would be treated like morons. All Vietnam Veterans Project 100,000 and regular veterans alike were faced with an insensitive Veterans Administration, which was desperately trying to deny the full scope of the damages done. The Veterans Administration kept us from getting fair disability compensation under Title 38 of the US code, by keeping us ignorant of our illnesses and injuries connected to the Vietnam War.

It was only through dogged persistence that I learned of the causes of my suffering that were a direct result of my tour in Vietnam:

☐ Chronic encephalopathy (brain damage) with manifestations of cluster migraine headaches, dizziness, ocular imbalance, and loss of memory

☐ Post Traumatic Stress Disorder (PTSD)

☐ Depression

☐ Wounds to my right leg

☐ Amputation of my right ring finger, my right pinkie finger and the ankylosed joint on my middle finger

☐ Loss of use in my right hand

☐ Bilateral ruptured ear drums (meaning both ears)

☐ Brain concussion

☐ Compound skull fracture

☐ Hemorrhaging of my optic nerves, bilateral

☐ Blindness resulting in two transplanted lenses

☐ Ongoing inflammation in both eyes, which has further caused the deterioration of my vision

☐ Irritable bowel syndrome

☐ Immunodeficiency

☐ Skin rashes/lesions

☐ Thyroid dysfunction

☐ Side-effects from steroids

☐ Colon spasms

☐ Multiple tumors and sarcoidosis

☐ Sarcoid rheumatoid arthritis

The Veterans Administration did not consider these problems to be not disabling, and some of the medical issues they considered less than severe enough to rate total disability. To add insult to injury, the Social Security Administration based their denial of my social security disability claim on the same denial of the Veterans Administration.

My psychological evaluation has provided an understanding of the mental wounds I received. So-called experts told me that these wounds to my psyche were not severe. For example, reports dated November 3 and 17 1981 contained the following evaluations:

> "He experienced psychological symptoms of a post-traumatic stress disorder, including startle reaction, intrusive thoughts and recollections, flash-backs, and a profound alienation from society. A day does not go by that he does not think about Vietnam, nor do many nights go by without a bad dream or a waking nightmare. The frequency and intensity are declining somewhat, but they still are common. Loud noises evoke a "startle reaction," or a self-protective reflex that would be appropriate in a combat situation, but are set off by sounds of civilian life, which mimic explosions, such as a car backfiring, a loud door slamming, or the fireworks on the Fourth of July. Sometimes these sounds have elicited a "flash-back," where he has a recurrent feeling that he is in Vietnam at the time, and takes "cover" behind a car, or hits the pavement, or other appropriate reactions to a combat situation. During the daytime when he has recollections, these sometimes become so real that for a moment he believes he is in Vietnam. Several times, he has had nightmares where he got out of bed and engaged in self-protective or combative behavior, including once striking a woman friend in his bed. As

soon as he woke up, he came to. Although he has never attempted suicide, Mr. Ward has often contemplated it, and even has a "suicide kit," a combination of various pills he has been prescribed that would be sufficient should he reach a point where he can't take it anymore.

"It is very common for persons who have undergone psychological traumas, as did Mr. Ward in Vietnam, to withdraw from normal social relationships and to be emotionally inhibited. This is certainly true in his case. However, much in truth, Mr. Ward was mistreated or neglected by various institutions since his return from Vietnam, what stands out from the psychological data is that he has more or less seized on this perceived victim role and lives it in a narrow and rigid way. As I mentioned above, it happens to parallel his personality pre-disposition. It is quite remarkable that a man with an already short fuse should have to endure the multiple discomforts, pain and limitation of his various physical problems, as well as the perceived humiliation of not getting his "due" from society. It is remarkable that he is still alive and has not either killed himself or gotten killed because of the tremendous tensions. I am not surprised that he has gotten into verbal and physical conflicts. The problem arises of accounting for his still being alive or outside of jail, which I account for by virtue of his narcissistic qualities. Specifically, I mean his very high regard for himself and his future, which motivates him to stay out of trouble. But I think his margin is running very thin there, and if there is not some kind of clarification in the near future, he just might "explode." Violence is not an easy thing to predict, but it does have a high probability of stress disorder; his personality disorder has just made it harder for him to cope

"Residual Functioning: It strikes me that Mr. Ward's physical ailments might be in themselves sufficient to make him totally disabled occupationally, but that is outside my area of expertise. His psychological reactions to his physical disability, as well as to the psychological stress of combat and undergoing life-threatening experiences, are of a moderate to severely disabling severity. The combination of his depression (specifically his low energy, inability to concentrate, low interest, dejection, and pessimism), general apprehensiveness, and restlessness, alienation from society, intense resentment, and profound impatience and hostility, would make him ill-suited for occupational adjustment. I think he would not attend consistently, and that if on a job, his work quality would be very erratic. He would not be able to deal with normal frustrations and production pressures, and would be extremely prone to get into conflicts with authorities and co-workers over the slightest irritation. If he could not leave the job to avoid a physical conflict, a fight would be sure to erupt. At this point, I think the only thing Mr. Ward can really do is take care of himself, and he can only do that marginally well. He is prone to resort to drugs and alcohol to cope with emotional stress and losses of self-esteem, which only worsen his prognosis. Were his physical problems to be resolved, he should be re-evaluated, because I expect that the stress level would go down significantly. But he would (need) months or years after the war. I am speaking of Post Traumatic Stress Disorders (PTSD). For those who were not in the situation and experiencing the horror personally, on an intimate level, it is hard to understand the deep psychological effects of killing another human being. Even though we were taught to see them as an impersonal, all-evil, must-be-destroyed, should-be-destroyed-enemy, the effects were enormous. To kill a man, woman or child at any time is intolerable to one's basic humanity. Hearing it is repugnant, seeing it is sickening, and doing it has proven to be fatally traumatic to the psyche. Other veterans, me included, suffer from overexposure to the rawness of having lived this experience. For me, the first time experience with the deaths was so stunning that I was unable to eat. I was scared to death."

That "Gung-ho fire" that I had from the psychological indoctrination during basic training had lost all meaning. I don't know what broke the stupor, but I attribute some responsibility to my having become somewhat combat hardened, if there is such a thing. Killing and witnessing death gory and bloody disrupts one's body chemistry; it literally left a bad taste in my mouth. Whatever was going on in my mind had manifested into things that happened to me physically, as well.

Some of my physical problems are a direct result of my psyche responding to the haunting pains and visions of pains, which have burned a permanent brand in my mind. This is one of the saddest things I have endured. I felt nothing good, except for the thankfulness of being alive. I would often wonder if I was still in one piece and dreaming or if I was hurt and just couldn't feel it.

The portrayed images on TV and movies are not an accurate picture of the fearful environment that surrounded us in Vietnam. The heroes I saw in Vietnam were of such, only because their lives depended on it. They were afraid, just like me. The pictures of death have never left me, and I continue to use those memories as an incentive to stay as far away as possible from conflict and death. It is sometimes hard to bear, but I must always continue to pursue a peaceful, non-violent life. For me, anything less is unthinkable and irrational, not to mention detrimental to the heath and emotional well-being I've managed to reestablish, to a certain degree.

My greatest wish is that the past and all the problems would just go away and let me live a normal life. But I know this will be with me forever. I live with the fear of possibly having to kill again, and I try my hardest to avoid any madness in society and my daily life, so as not to awaken this insanity inside me.

I think one of the reasons that so many of my comrades are in self-imposed isolation, inhibited in a crowd, and wary of the general population is that avoidance of violence. Killing is supposed to be socially unacceptable, but it is quite difficult to separate what must be done in war, and what should not be done in civilian life. The lack of understanding and compassion, coupled with the multitude of disappointments from our government, don't do much to help combat veterans readapt to the environment of home.

For me, the task of turning off the killing machine I knew so well was a constant struggle. The indoctrination of the Gung-Ho Marine Corps was "kill, kill, kill," and that was the approved thing to do. You add that to the practical application of a year in combat, where the concept of killing went from talk to the real thing, and it increases the pervasive threat of losing control. Therefore, back in civilized society, when placed in a hostile situation, it was hard not to exhibit these skills. Re-adjustment required a lot more preparation than what was given to us. We have many tragic results from those Vietnam veterans who could not find a way to restrain themselves.

Those who are left to deal with PTSD endure a lifetime of coping with the ever-haunting fears of flashbacks. Without proper treatment, the only resort is to self-medicate with alcohol, drugs, and for some, suicide. The things in life that are normal for some people are triggers for many combat veterans. A common thing, like rain, can easily awaken traumatic combat experiences that one suffered during the monsoon season in Vietnam. Fast moving automobiles can sound like incoming artillery. Without help, there is no hope for so many veterans. Thus, self-inflicted violence, or violence toward other, can prevail. Self-inflicted violence is not just suicide, but can be things like isolation, hunger (searching garbage cans for food), and self-mutilation. Police officers are often given disability compensation for one-time exposure to traumatic encounters, as are civilians, while we veterans are faced with repeated and often daily traumatic life-threatening experiences. Our exposure seemed to go by without any interest.

An awareness of Post-Traumatic Stress Disorder and how it affected post-war veterans during those early years following their return to civilian life would have saved many of them from an ill fate, I'm sure. The more I learned and understood about PTSD, the better I was able to pursue methods of coping. However, I did not understand it in time to save my own marriage, which took place in 1968 after I had returned home, wounded. The marriage lasted only a year. Through my marriage, I also began to understand the ignorance of those who didn't understand. The many broken families, employment problems, and problems readjusting to civilian life would not have taken such a tragic toll in the veteran community if PTSD had been treated, rather than ignored. Left untreated, flashbacks take these veterans mentally and emotionally back to those horrible experiences of war and its realities, years later. We must understand that incidents of flashbacks have caused tragedies to the veterans and to others who have been innocents. Flashbacks are also known to affect those who suffer from them. They produce horrors in the veterans, which often leave them removed from acceptance of authority and not able to go through life as a normal person. This can also produce the walking time bomb, which has reared its ugly head repeatedly, bringing about more casualties. There are those who were less than capable of coping with the rigors of training, let alone the combat arenas. They didn't have a chance from the start. Many who remain out there are neglected and ticking. Thus, the war goes on.

Those of us who are fortunate enough to be alive still are a testament to the success of our having no other choice but to help ourselves. We have had to enact what we deemed was the best way under our individual circumstances just to survive. We have self-medicated and self-preserved ourselves just enough to be still alive. So many Vietnam veterans opted for the PTSD program at the Veteran Mental Health Clinic. The drugs administered even Thorazine, with what I consider ill effects still possibly could have saved many of those who opted, through no fault of their own, for suicide.

PTSD left many Vietnam Veterans psychologically damaged. But, we were faced with other health problems just as damaging physically and psychologically. To have any disease, which is classified "incurable," has been mentally, as well as physically, disturbing. One of the most prevalent fears we Vietnam veterans had was of contracting what they called black syphilis. During our indoctrination, we were forewarned of the problem related to sexually transmitted diseases. Our trainers told us that black syphilis was incurable and left us with the question of what happened to those who were exposed. What classification would be entered on one's records, and where would they ultimately end up? Would our government allow such infected persons to return to the population at large? Would these soldiers be awarded Purple Hearts for being wounded in battle? Or would they be classified as missing in action while they were held in exile?

I wondered what happened to these veterans; the combat veteran who fought next to me, the guy I befriended, the warrior I didn't even know, the people who I didn't have a problem with until I came home. I wondered about the military experiences that came home with us, and which we continually relived. The life we have left after the trauma of the war is almost guaranteed to be haunted and hurtful until the end.

These effects may not be the same for all vets, since it is an emotional thing that varies from soldier to soldier. However, in my case, it all seemed to be a horrible thing. Close fighting tends to stick to one's soul in a more traumatic way. There seems to be more shock involved; things happen so fast amid chaos and confusion. I don't think anyone can easily shed these encounters because of the fear and the stunning reality. The horrid circumstances leave a lifetime of impressions that are a constant aggravation, which will last forever. It is no matter that it was supposed to be a wartime effort. It is not conducive to living peacefully and contentedly back in civilian life, after seeing young kids, women, and old people trying to kill you, while you are trying to kill them. To the contrary, it is a detriment to peaceful living, since I could find no justification for having to kill someone in a far-off land who I had no problem with.

Chapter 7

HERBICIDES IN VIETNAM

In addition to the actual wounds and the PTSD, there were diseases that crept up on many vets, leaving our emotional, physical, and spiritual health shattered. I refer to the a medical condition attributed to exposure to herbicides. I had strange bumps that itched severely and inflamed my face, head, neck, and hands. I had problems with my digestive track that I had never experienced before Vietnam. I could see that Vietnam had given me with thousands of other veterans these strange, new experiences, which we didn't understand or know anything about. It took me six years to find out anything about Agent Orange, and to realize that this highly toxic poison was most likely the culprit for my skin rashes and other chronic conditions. My exposure to this toxin directly affected my ability to live a normal and healthy life.

One condition that is attributed to the exposure to herbicides is peripheral neuropathy. The advisory committee for Agent Orange found that there was a significant statistical association between this disorder and exposure to dioxin. The committee members indicated that other factors that they must consider regarding with nervous and uncontrollable tics are the patient's age and whether the individual suffers from other known causes of peripheral neuropathy, such as diabetes, alcoholism, or Guillain-Barré syndrome. The committee advised that the disorder would manifest within ten years of the last known dioxin exposure. This committee didn't arrive at this ten-year deal until 1991. That was quite late to be of any help to those who suffer from the problem. It merely illustrates how the VA avoided the responsibility to compensate those who suffer from Agent Orange and other herbicidal exposure.

On March 29, 1991, the Department of the Air Force released study results that indicated a significant association between dioxin levels and lipid-related death indicators. Specifically, diabetes and body fat were associated with dioxin levels. Cholesterol and other related serum lipid levels also were significantly associated with dioxin poisoning.

All of these conditions, especially peripheral neuropathy, which is a nervous system condition, cause physical numbness and weakness. Of course, if the veteran didn't realize what the problem was or was not properly diagnosed as has normally been the case within ten years of their exposure, they would just be out of luck. How can the government study something for twenty-five years before coming to a decision that, yes, it would be accepted as a service connected disability? After making such a decision far too late to save the lives of so many veterans, how could that same government have the audacity to determine that someone should have diagnosed the veterans within ten years of exposure for it to count as service-related? Administration medical staff members were not even allowed to mention the words, "Agent Orange," and they definitely weren't allowed to diagnose anything related to herbicide exposure.

What a game they play. I personally have suffered from the symptoms of peripheral neuropathy and I have continued to do so since the war. Scientists began to study these problems because of the numerous complaints upon the immediate return of veterans. Then, after all those years of study, the VA decided it was actually service connected. They agreed that those exposures should be considered service connected, but only if the veterans could show that the symptoms existed within ten years of the discharge.

On July 27, 1993, the National Academy of Sciences (NAS) Institute of Medicine's Committee to Review the Health Effects in Vietnam Veterans of Exposure to Herbicides released its initial findings. The Committee found "sufficient evidence" to conclude that there is a positive association between herbicides and (1) soft tissue sarcoma, (2) non-Hodgkin's lymphoma, (3) Hodgkin's disease, (4) chlorachne and (5) porphyria cutanea tarda (in genetically susceptible individuals).

The Committee also found "limited/suggestive evidence" of an association between exposure to herbicides used in Vietnam and three other types of cancer: respiratory cancers (including lung, larynx, and trachea), prostate cancer, and multiple myeloma.

For most conditions reviewed, the Committee concluded that there was "inadequate/insufficient evidence" to determine whether an association exists between spray and exposure to the poisons. The NAS Committee included the following diseases and disorders were in this third category:

☐ Hepatobiliary cancers(including liver, gall bladder, and bile ducts)
☐ Nasal/nasopharyngeal cancer
☐ Bone cancer
☐ Female reproductive cancers (breast, cervical)
☐ Testicular cancer
☐ Leukemia
☐ Spontaneous abortion

☐ Birth defects
☐ Neonatal/infant death and stillbirths
☐ Low birth weight
☐ Childhood cancer in offspring
☐ Abnormal sperm parameters and infertility
☐ Cognitive and neuropsychiatric disorders
☐ Motor/coordination dysfunction
☐ Peripheral nervous system disorders
☐ Metabolic and digestive disorders (diabetes, changes in liver enzymes, lipid abnormalities, ulcers)
☐ Immune system disorders
☐ Respiratory disorders

For a small group of cancers, the Committee found "limited/suggested evidence" that there is "no association" with herbicides used in Vietnam. This category included skin cancer, gastrointestinal tumors (stomach cancer, pancreatic cancer, colon cancer, and rectal cancer), bladder cancer, and brain tumors. The Committee report noted, however, that even for these conditions, "the possibility of a very small elevation in risk at the levels of exposure studied can never be excluded."

2It is known that from January 1962 to February 1971, the estimated quantities of herbicides and TCDD disseminated in South Vietnam was 106,763,260 pounds; and that between January 1965 and February 1971,

2 Young, A. L., J. A. Calcagni, C. E. Thalken, *et al.* '*The Toxicology, Environmental Fate, and Human Risk of Herbicide Orange and Its Associated Dioxin*' (Washington, D.C.: The Surgeon General, United States Air Force. 1978), p. I-28.

117,712,860 gallons of Agent Orange, 5,239,853 gallons of Agent White, and 2,161,456 gallons of Agent Blue were disseminated in South Vietnam, then one gets some rough idea of the scope of the severe and fatal health problem this caused the Vietnam Vet.

ESTIMATED QUANTITIES OF INDIVIDUAL CHEMICALS SPRAYED IN SOUTH VIETNAM

SUMMARY

The choice of herbicides used in South Vietnam in Operation RANCH HAND, 1962-1971, was based upon those herbicides that had been widely used in world agriculture, shown to be effective in controlling abroad spectrum of vegetation and proven sage to humans and animals. The major herbicides used in South Vietnam were phenoxy herbicides 2,4-D and 2,4,5-T. These two herbicides were formulated as water insoluble and code-named by the military as Purple, Orange, Pink, and Green. A water soluble amine formulation of 2,4-D was used in Herbicide White. Two other herbicides were extensively used by the military, picloram (in White) and cacodylic acid (in Blue).

An estimated 107 million pounds of herbicides were aerially disseminated on 6 million acres in South Vietnam from January 1962 through February 1971. Approximately 94 percent of all herbicides sprayed in Vietnam were 2,4-D (56 million pounds or 53 percent of total) or 2,4,5-T (44 million pounds or 41 percent of total. The 44 million pounds of 2,4,5-T contained an estimated 368 lb of the toxic contaminant, 2,3,7,8-tetrachlorodibenzo-p dioxin (TCDD or dioxin). Ninety-six percent of all 2,4,5-T was contained in Herbicide Orange; Ninety-six percent of all 2,4,5-T was contained in Herbicide Orange; the remaining 4 percent in Herbicides Green, Pink, and Purple. However, Herbicides Green, Pink, and Purple contained approximately 40 percent of the estimated amount of TCDD disseminated in South Vietnam.

Green, Pink, and Purple were sprayed as defoliants on less than 90,000 acres from 1962 through 1964, a period when only a small force of U.S. military personnel where in South Vietnam. Ninety percent of all the Herbicide Orange (containing 38.3 million pounds of 2,4,5-T and 203 ob of TCDD) were used in defoliation operations on 2.9 million acres of inland forests and mangrove forests of South Vietnam.

The handling, transport, and storage procedures employed for the herbicides generally precluded physical contact with the herbicides by most military personnel assigned to Operation RANCH HAND. However, flight mechanics (console operators for the internal spray systems) were the most likely military personnel exposed to the herbicides.

The methods employed in spraying the herbicides and the geographical areas designated for dissemination of the herbicides generally precluded direct physical contact with the herbicide by military personnel assigned to other military programs.

Chapter 8

WAR PROTEST

One of the major facts of life facing the Vietnam veteran coming home was war protests. No war in the history of US warfare was protested as much as was the Vietnam conflict.

Upon my return to the states, I found a strange coincidence. Robert Kennedy had been against the war in Vietnam and the processes used to amass the troops. With all the chaos that was happening during this period, including labor strikes and street battles waged against the Johnson Administration, it led me to think that there was more to the Robert Kennedy assassination than has been said. I have my doubts. The Johnson Administration seemed eager to silence those who would protest going to war. Those who knew about the process used to get the troops there were apparently dangerous, and those who shared that knowledge with the public were a threat to the recruiting efforts of the administration. Could there be more to the Robert Kennedy assassination? No other administration has had by so much tragedy surrounding it in the history of this country, to my knowledge.

May I remind you that the Johnson Administration went all out to keep down the protests, locking up draft card burners and flag burners? They discredited famed and noted people who stood against their war policies, such as Muhammad Ali. The administration called him a communist or a communist sympathizer, doing all they could to keep their "police action" going.

Numerous youth were subjected to penalties of jail time or were given the option of serving military time after burning their draft cards. Despite objections and anti-war sentiment from high-ranking congressmen, senators, and famous actors, in addition to protests from the poor, middle class, and wealthy citizens alike, this administration continued to press the war. They did almost everything possible to uphold their less than honorable pursuit of war, and to kill off our youth for the benefit of the big money interests. All scruples were thrown out to meet their ends. Dissidents began to react with the fury and wrath toward the system and took their protests to the streets.

The years passed and the protesting continued as the body bags and wounded continued to pile up. It became apparent that more was needed to derail this ill-fated "police action." Nevertheless, the Johnson Administration kept up its fervor in recruiting, drafting, and pushing into the combat arena all of these less than qualified or ineligible youths, to face the elements of madness some ten thousand miles away from home. The so-called Moron Corps grew larger, despite the protests, and maybe because of them. The more intellectual American young people could see clearly that this was a dishonorable and disgraceful war, for which they wanted no part.

The administration's choice to lower enlistment standards, forced those of us subjected to comply. This was not a "government of the people," but the beginnings of a war "regardless of the people." I agree that the government should be able to use the draft, as long as it is the choice of the people, and as long as it conforms to our chosen constitutional standards. Primarily, congressional approval is in order and anything less as in the case of Vietnam has produced a cornucopia of pain, disparities, and life-ending problems.

One of the most noted incidents was the horrible response toward the protests and burning of draft cards at Kent State University in Ohio. In that incident, our own troops in the National Guard shot and killed seven white students. These students were not armed, but they were simply exercising their right to disagree and protest, as was given in our constitution. This example shows how adamant the Johnson Administration was to squash opposition to their war efforts. Another historic response was the way they stripped Muhammad Ali of his heavyweight championship title and they attempted to shame and disgrace him publicly. This was done to answer him exercising his constitutional right to refuse to take the life of another unjustly, and thus violate his religious beliefs as a minister of the Muslim faith, which conformed to the policy of conscientious objector. Military officials ultimately sought to get Muhammad Ali as a Project 100,000 case, because he had failed miserably at the Army mental examination. But the famed boxer fought that in court, and his case was later upheld by the US Supreme Court.

Little did we know while we were in the thick of the fighting, that black leaders were also heavily protesting the Vietnam War. The media tended to depict black people in the Civil Rights battle and white people in the antiwar movement. Black opposition to the American policy in Southeast Asia set a precedent, because historically, black people have sought to fully participate as fighting men and for their rights as American citizens on a par equal to any other American citizen. Black Americans had taken part in all of the wars of this country, while also enduring unequal treatment, segregation, humiliation, and injustice.

I believe that most black people could feel this plight

clearly, despite media images of black men who were serving and dying in this war. The numbers of dying black men was far disproportionate to their numbers in the American population by a whole. They knew that not only was this unfair, but it represented a shameful act on the part of our government.

Of all the black leaders, Dr. Martin Luther King Jr.'s opposition to the war had the most resounding impact. King was the number one thorn in the side of the Johnson Administration, reminding the mighty warmonger of the horrendous immoral inadequacies of their policies. He pointed out the injustice of using underprivileged, under-qualified societal rejects the poor blacks, Mexicans, Native Americans, and poor whites to feed the irrational frenzy of war. King delivered his most vitriolic attack on the war in Vietnam aimed at on the Johnson Administration in a speech called, A Time to Break Silence. When delivering this historic speech at the Riverside Church in New York City on April 4, 1967, King stated:

> "As I have walked among the desperate, rejected and angry young men, I have told them that Molotov cocktails and rifles would not solve their problems. I have tried to offer them my deepest compassion while maintaining my conviction that social change comes most meaningfully through non-violent action. But they asked and rightly so what about Vietnam? They asked if our own nation wasn't using massive doses of violence to solve its problems, to bring about the changes it wanted. Their questions hit home, and I knew that I could never again raise my voice against the violence of the oppression in the ghettos without having

first spoken clearly to the greatest purveyor
of violence in the world today my own
government.

For the sake of those boys, for the sake of this government,
the sake of the hundreds of thousands trembling under our
violence, I cannot be silent."

King was well aware of the plight of the black man in
Vietnam. He stated at a peace rally in Beverly Hills, California,
February 25, 1967:

"We are willing to make the Negro 100
percent of a citizen in warfare, but reduce him
to 50 percent of a citizen on American soil. Half
of all Negroes live in substandard housing and
he has half the income as whites. There is twice
as much unemployment and infant mortality
among Negroes, there were twice as many
Negroes in combat in Vietnam at the beginning
of 1967, and twice as many died in action (20.6
percent) in proportion to their numbers in the
population as whites."

Dr. King's expressions of utter disdain for the illegal and
unacceptable approach to filling the military ranks with poor
black men purely to gain cannon fodder for the most protested
war (police action) in the history of this country instilled hostility
in the Johnson Administration. Dr. King's success with the civil
rights movement was not what cost him his life. It appears to
me that what eventually took his life was his intrusion into the
flow of the war effort and the possible re-election of the Johnson
Administration. This double threat of anti-war sentiment and
re-election doubts was a result of the embarrassment, ridicule,

and shame illustrated by an esteemed leader, which made the public aware of the Johnson Administration's misdoings. In my personal opinion, King's opposition to the Vietnam War was the catalyst that took his life. Was it a coincidence that he was killed at the height of his war protestation and not during his protest for civil rights? Was it a coincidence that he was murdered one year, almost to the day, after he had given his historic speech, A Time to Break Silence?

The battles in the streets were waged throughout the war in Vietnam. The citizen protests during this time helped. Dr. Martin Luther King Jr. and all those who protested the war held that the number of the war deaths was 58,000.

I now wish that Americans would fight to stop our current post-war negligence, particularly the death toll of Vietnam veterans' suicides, numbering more the 100,000. I hope to bring attention to the problems plaguing the Vietnam veterans to this day. Just as your protests made the end of the war in Vietnam happen, further protests can elicit fair and just treatment of the Vietnam heroes. We veterans need help to bring us up from alienation, and at least to try to make an effort to redeem from further suffering. The protests needed now should be to correct the injustices that have been made and that continue to haunt the Vietnam vet and his enjoyment of being an American.

American acceptance and reconciliation with Vietnam vets occurred in the 80s and 90s, and the general public sentiment now is that the vet is honored for service. Certainly, that was not the case during the war or immediately following. It might be wise to acknowledge that the public's opinion of the Vietnam vet changed from negative to positive.

The media exposure to the problems of Vietnam veterans throughout the years have left a lot to be desired. However, Mr. Ted Turner and others have taken an interest. Mr. Turner has been the most prolific. More interest from those in a position to do so would be a great help to struggling veterans.

It takes We the People!

Chapter 9

READJUSTMENT TO CIVILIAN LIFE

When I felt like I was well enough to go home on leave for the first time, my agenda was in the following order: sex, fun, and marriage. This is exactly what took place, including the unfortunate marriage. Then, I would be off to Camp Pendleton, California for further treatment and processing out of the military. During my processing out, which took some six to eight months, three white corporals who had served in Vietnam at the same time as me were promoted, while I was denied. I couldn't understand how this could happen so overtly. I felt highly insulted at this outwardly racist move and took immediate action. I went to the higher-ranking battalion commander in protest of my white company commander's refusal to promote me to sergeant. I had earned the right to be promoted, and I was going to fight for it

My captain was a tall white Iowan, who exhibited racial preferences toward whites, and against blacks. He promoted two white marines who had lower qualifying scores than any of the blacks. The two white marines protested to the captain, but to no avail. Gunnery Sgt. Wright was a black man, and he refused to admit that there was anything wrong with the captain's racism. The black sergeant was protecting himself instead of us. He was a true sellout.

As it happened, the battalion commander had problems with this refusal and reversed the captain's decision, thus authorizing my promotion to sergeant. My promotion to sergeant meant more to me than just the additional stripe and the raise in pay. It had meaning to me because, despite being a Project 100,000 recruit a member of the so-called Moron Corps I had earned it. What was also important was that they based my retirement pay on my pay grade when discharged. The three white Marines who were promoted ahead of me all told me that they had protested to my captain about the unfairness of his action, but this didn't change his decision. It helped to know that they were on my side. But as it turned out, I was released from active duty before I could be promoted to sergeant.

A black gunnery sergeant had gone along with the decision of the captain who had denied me the promotion, because he worked for the captain. This added insult to injury, and before leaving the base, I was audacious enough to face him one on one and rub his "Uncle Tom" attitude with my strongest resentment. Before leaving the base for indefinite leave, I had rejected an offer of ten thousand dollars severance pay, and requested a hearing by the Board of Medical Review. In this hearing, I was granted a retirement with full benefits, privileges, and a forty-percent disability rating. I was disappointed by this, because I believe I should have been given a higher disability rating. This was especially considering the wounds that I suffered during the war. My disappointment had an apparent down-sliding affect on my state of mind. In my naiveté, I ignored these incidents as omens of things to come, and went off into the world to chase my utopia.

I was discharged to Oakland, California, to wait for my processing into retirement. It seemed the proper time to get busy with finding a job and to start enjoying my life again. As it happened, the only immediate work available was pumping gas, which I jumped on as a stepping-stone until better things happened. After all, I was a disabled, honorably discharged, combat veteran, and like other vets, this had to count for something.

During the course of my transition back to civilian life, something strange began to happen. My face broke out with an odd rash of bumps. These bumps were filled with liquid, and they would erupt and weep. Then the bumps would crust over with scab that resembled clear plastic it was unlike anything I had ever seen. This struck me as being too different to be normal. I went to the naval hospital where the doctors gathered around me in a quiet discussion that didn't include me, and diagnosed me with a rash with unknown etiology. They said it was probably caused from shaving. I thought this was strange, and it didn't sit right with my better judgment. However, I did as the doctors prescribed. I took the tetracycline and cool wet soaks, as ordered. I assumed they knew what they were doing.

I then began to notice other issues. I noticed that my stomach was giving me problems again. The doctors suggested that it was possible ulcers. My head wound began dominating my attention, and I started to experience dizziness, an upset stomach, and instances of passing out. It made it very difficult to find activities that I could handle. But I told myself that this was a part of what I had to endure while recovering.

Through all this, the rashes kept returning. With that came chronic itching, weeping, and scabbing over with the same consistency as before. The rash appeared on my head, on my neck and in my genital area, obviously not a result of shaving. I then started to wonder if something in my body was moving around and erupting. This led me to believe, and fear, that it could erupt in a vital organ, and cause major problems, including life-threatening dangers. But I kept going along with the doctors. I always had doubts about whether or not the VA had diagnosed and treated me properly. These problems had already begun to interrupt my employment capabilities, with the frequency of the eruptions, headaches, and dizziness, aside from the stomach problems.

In 1970, the US Postal Service hired me as a mail sorter. During this time, I began to notice strange feelings or nervousness. I began to experience nightmares with cold sweats, and I was in a state of confusion. I really didn't know what to make of it, other than the thought that it was a normal reaction to recovering from my wounds, and that these symptoms would likely go away in time.

As my ailments got worse, I began having problems with a particular supervisor at the post office. He told me that he really didn't care about any of my problems, and he talked down to me with considerable rudeness. He continued to do this for quite a while. Besides all of my physical problems, I felt as though this man was intimidating me and I began to take serious offence. This led me to begin making plans of how to take him out, which was how I had handled problem people in Vietnam. I went so far as to find out where he lived and plotted a covert operation to remove him. As it happened, I chose instead to get away from the situation, to avoid losing it and killing him.

My consciousness of killing was not a problem for me, since I had grown somewhat accustomed to that while serving in Vietnam. What restrained me was my struggle to resume a normal life. I had difficulty pursuing peace and contentment, which was what I considered normal.

I didn't know anything about stress. In my youth, since I grew up in a racist environment, instances of stressful experiences were commonplace. Now that I was learning more about it, I began to understand what was happening to me. But I still didn't have the knowledge or ability needed to handle it.

During this period, my wife and I went through numerous problems. She could not comprehend what I had suffered. No person, without the firsthand exposure to such horrific circumstances, could understand. Along with my struggle to adapt to the real world, burdened with a mental handicap, with my physical problems, and with social and racial disparities, my wife and I also had several miscarried pregnancies. Everything in our lives was tumbling around us and eventually we parted ways.

I was a mess as I trotted along, trying to find myself, and my direction. It became an even more difficult task then. It recently dawned on me that I had been quite naïve with my past idealism. I thought that if I had served my country faithfully, I would be deserving of the good life that America offered. I soon learned that nobody really cared. This fact became apparent to many Vietnam vets soon after returning home, when they had their hopes for the American dream dashed. To me, it was clear that I had to call on all the resources I could, and disregard what others had deemed the norm. Survival with what I had left was my utmost priority.

I had originally challenged the Marine Corps regarding my promotion to sergeant. The commander agreed to promote me, but I was released before the promotion was in effect. I decided that I had to take steps to rectify this mistake. I started by requesting a copy of my records pertaining to that promotion. Sure enough, the authorization for the promotion was in the records. From there, I requested from the Board of Correction of Naval Records to make the proper changes and pay me retroactively in accordance. This was done, and I define that moment as the beginning of my fight for the benefits due to me as a disabled Vietnam veteran and against the injustices done to me. This led me to realize the lack of respect and concern for the Vietnam veterans.

I invested some fifteen years trying to survive after Vietnam. As a rule, all of my endeavors were on again, off again. My attempts to further my education were a challenge; studying and controlling the stress while getting back into civilian life. I stuck with college for three years, even making the dean's list, before leaving because of my ailments. I turned to the Veteran's Administration for help.

In 1979, I filed for veterans disability benefits. The process exasperated my already troubled state of mind, with too many snags, bureaucratic twists, curves, and delays. In the process of this new fight with the Veterans Administration system, I got involved with the California Veterans Coalition. This Coalition had been defunded because of their candidness in pursuing changes in the Veterans Administration's Department of Labor. Veterans have challenged the VA's lack of conforming to the laws governing their responsibility to Vietnam and disabled veterans.

My interest in the lack of service to the veterans became obsessive. I was prepared to suffer whatever wrath or repercussions, which may come from my fight for the benefits these veterans truly deserved. I began to apply what few abilities I had to learning all that I possibly could about Title 38 of the US Code, (veteran's benefits). The harm caused as the result of the Veterans Administration's failure to address the needs, concerns, and problems of the veterans who they were mandated to help became clear to me. [3]An article by Joshua Kors titled, "How the VA Abandons Our Vets," published in 2008, in The Nation magazine supports my assertion regarding the VA. While the article is not about abuse of Vietnam veterans, but rather addressed problems for Gulf War veterans, it is disturbing that nothing has changed in the intervening decades between the conflict I was in and the current war.

After witnessing many veterans with too many of the same problems, I felt the need to stand up for our rights that were enacted by congressionally mandated laws. That is the reason I took on this responsibility to get the benefits we deserved.

While wrestling with the establishment, I discovered things about my medical disabilities that were new to me. I would never have received treatment for these disabilities if I had not raised the issues vehemently. I knew that I had a head injury, but I wasn't told about the brain damage (encephalopathy) with the manifestation of headaches, dizziness, and ocular imbalance. The mental disorder known as Post Traumatic Stress Disorder (PTSD) was never mentioned, nor treated.

My knowledge of Agent Orange didn't come to the forefront until I became a member of the Agent Orange Committee at the University of California in Berkeley. That is when it dawned on me, through information obtained from toxicologists on the committee, that I carried some of the symptoms of toxic poisoning. The skin rashes were similar to the symptoms of chloracne, and my digestive and colon problems which were never be explained and had been described as having no etiology were actually caused by something else.

My eyes had been doing crazy things. I was having vision problems, headaches, dizziness, and spells of passing out, accompanied by colon spasms, diarrhea, and vomiting. When I became aware that the Veterans Administration knew this, I became most irate in the presence of these people. My brothers were undoubtedly going through the same madness. I could understand now why so many veterans had given up on hassling with the system, and had gone off to exist the best way they could.

At that point, I applied to the Board of Veterans Appeal, in Washington, for the right to represent veteran's claims and was approved for the work. I became an official veterans' agent, officially allowing me to represent veterans in their fight for justice. Armed with this, I went about the arduous task of doing what I could to see that some veterans got their just due.

There was one instance where the Director of the Veterans Administration in San Francisco informed me that he didn't have to talk to me regarding anything. At this point, I presented him with the letter of approval to represent veteran's claims. This changed his attitude quickly. While in discussion with the director, he stated that, "If a veteran doesn't know, he doesn't get." He made this statement, not knowing that I would remember his words and write them here. His arrogance was only exceeded by his stupidity, and it showed what little interest he had in doing his job. This didn't come as a surprise to me, since I had already experienced the same negative demeanor when dealing with his underling counselors.

At another time, a counselor became belligerent when I asked him to repeat what he had said so that the veteran I was representing could understand it. The counselor started ranting and saying things like, "To hell with Congressman Dellums," alluding to the fact that the Congressman had been working with us to bring to light the injustices done to veterans. This counselor went on to insult Senator Allen Cranston and President Reagan. Not long after he went off, so did I. This was when the US Marshalls were called to quell me, which didn't do any good. The Assistant Director threatened that he would call in the FBI to calm me down, and this didn't do anything either. The rights of veterans and I were being violated, and I didn't give a... about any threats. With my actions that day, I was branded as another crazy veteran, suffering with PTSD and I didn't care about that either.

It was now becoming quite clear that numerous veterans were suffering the same, and in many cases, a worse fate than myself. The many crazy things that Vietnam veterans were doing became ever present in my thinking. It inspired me to learn as much as I could about their circumstances. In addition, I was determined to avoid the worst for myself. I had accepted that this could very well be an omen of bad things to come for me.

I became ever more bitter toward the system, and caused problems whenever confronted with the obtuse personnel of the Veterans Administration. At the various hospitals and outpatient clinics, belligerent uncaring attitudes were pervasive and I showed no tolerance whatsoever for the mistreatment of a veteran.

It was programmed in me at the young age of eighteen, that service in the armed forces and earning an honorable discharge would just about guarantee that I could get a good job and be held in high esteem, especially during war-times. Most of the Vietnam era youths also believed this to be true. In my experience with combat troops, it appeared that we all shared the same dreams as we returned to the real world. If we made it back, we held firm in our minds that everything would be good. In our naiveté, we thought we would be treated like heroes for having endured the madness of jungle warfare. In our optimistic views, we painted all kinds of mental pictures of good lives that we hoped to one-day lead. Everyone was going to do well from then on, because we knew that all Americans would appreciate our sacrifices. They would know what we had faced, and would give us a warm welcome home. After all, we had come from the land of plenty and opportunity, even though most of us came from the ghettoes, small towns, and the criminal justice system.

First, on the guys' lists, was being able to sit on the toilet, read a paper, and come out when ready. Second, on the list was to take a long bath while enjoying the drink of your choice. Third was to have sex with all the girls in the world. Fourth, was to get a good job doing what you liked doing, getting a wonderful paycheck, and pursuing the American dream. The American dream entailed owning a home with a picket fence, a nice car, nice clothes, and a happy ending. While we thought, prayed, and dreamed of getting closer to our rotation date, we calendar scratched and discussed what we assumed would be our turn for the good life in the world. After Vietnam, many of those whom we fought for are now living the American Dream. They live the good life while the Vietnam warriors still suffer from their injuries and are doomed to be denied assistance or a roof over their heads. So much money is going to everyone, but the heroes who have done the most and deserve the most, get the least. There seems to be a lack of understanding about who deserves to be helped and an apparent disdain for those who gave so much and received nothing for their sacrifice.

During the time when I was trying to take charge of my emotions, pains, and my state of confusion, I got lost in how to maintain the proper habits that would help me to keep a grip on my ever more repressive state of mind.

By constantly fighting for a sense of normalcy and in trying to feel better, many of us returned home only to face new challenges far beyond anything we were equipped mentally to handle or cope with. I went to the naval hospital with all of the problems that hurt me and even those that were tormenting my mental state. It was very hard for me to understand why doctors could do nothing about my rashes, which resembled something that one would imagine from a movie about a strange alien illness.

The scabs that were ever present on many parts of my body were so strange and obviously out of the ordinary. Of all the cuts and scrapes that I have ever experienced, these were above and beyond the norm.

The naval hospital doctors always concluded that there was no etiology for the origins of these problems. I often felt like there was information that they were not truthful with me about, and they were leaving me to rot on the vine.

All of this motivated me to try anything possible to alleviate the constant hardships I was just trying to rehabilitate myself within what now was an entirely new and strange society from what I expected, a society that really didn't care what happened to me. At the time, it seemed to me that oppression and JIM CROW was haunting me all along.

Having to face the reality that my life was truly going to be this way, I sought and found places to hide. I used the shelter of women, alcohol, and street drugs to cope with my new reality. After successfully being able to avoid all of these things in my youth, I succumbed then, just as so many other veterans did for self-medication.

When there is the perception that everything is failing, it's quite easy to abandon normal discipline and seek help in other ways.

During my trip through the abyss of drug use, there was always the further aggravation of the problems from the Veterans Administration refusing to help and their continuing onslaught of denial around every corner.

No matter the evidence, their first ruling was always that the veteran was not encumbered or disabled. These denials were accompanied by the same attitude from the Social Security Administration. It was a classic paradox; I was only disabled if the Veterans Administration said so, and their policy was to never say so.

I and many other veterans were and still are caught in the teeth of this conspiracy between government agencies to evade their duties, because the veterans aren't worthy and it's not cost effective to service many disabled and dysfunctional veterans.

In the process of my addiction, I was fortunate to have the

wherewithal to maintain a discipline and respect for myself, and not do many of the things that are motivated by the addiction, such as criminal behavior or self-destruction. My self-discipline and self-respect eventually led me back to sanity and civil reason.

For me, drug problems were not the thing that induced me to change. What happened was that after so long battling the Veterans Administration, I came across a doctor who made the decision that I should be totaled out (meaning he classified me as 100 percent disabled.) He ordered me not to do anything that I didn't want to do, and to avoid all of those things that were irritating to me which triggered anxieties.

After receiving proper medications and care, I stopped the drugs cold turkey and have had a clean bill of health since.

Chapter 10

FIGHTING FOR AFFIRMATIVE ACTION

O verall, you should know that the warriors during the Vietnam crisis consisted of whites, blacks, Mexicans, Indians, Jews, and Asian Americans. Some soldiers were immigrants who gained their citizenship through joining the military. All of these people have suffered from the lack of compliance to the Affirmative Action policies, specifically, the Vietnam Readjustment Act of 1972, Section 204.

The 1960s and 1970s were years when the people of America fought back. Black people fought to break down the walls of segregation. Women were fighting for equal rights and equal opportunities. Americans of all colors and classes were fighting against the War in Vietnam.

During the years of the Vietnam conflict, there were 3,403,000 active US military personal stationed in the SE Asia theater (Vietnam, Laos, Cambodia.) Of these, 303,644 were wounded, and an additional 58,282 were killed. This represented an overall casualty rate of more than ten percent. This also represented a huge undertaking for the Veterans Administration, helping 3.4 million veterans. In light of these numbers, it may not be surprising that they developed policies to deny benefits initially, but that doesn't make it right. It is unconscionable that the care of these combat veterans was not a priority for our government.

I feel it is vitally necessary for Vietnam veterans to fight for all their rights, benefits, and entitlements, too. They needed to fight for two basic reasons. One was that if they did not fight for their own rights, they are not likely ever to get them. I learned this lesson painfully. The second reason is that if there was ever anyone who needed a cause to fight for, to stop focusing on depressing circumstances, and have something to channel their frustration, it is the Vietnam veteran. So many of these veterans, in particular, have committed suicide, because life has lost meaning to them. They have been made to feel by the country that they had fought for that they are useless and worthless. Despite my traumas and my wounds, I come from people who have always fought back. My psychological profile suggests that this tradition remained alive in me, even when I wanted nothing more than to retreat from the world or give up.

I learned much about the plight of Vietnam veterans in general when I filed for veterans disability benefits and was denied most of my claims. With this, I became highly upset and disappointed, to say the least; but I did not do what the administration wanted me and other veterans to do Give Up. I vowed to continue to fight for my benefits, no matter how long it took.

To add insult to injury, the Social Security Administration based their denial of my social security disability benefit claim on the same denial made by the Veterans Administration.

The Regional offices of the Veterans Administration have the authority to resolve disability claims, but rarely do so, thus pushing the claimant to give up the pursuit. Many veterans are so encumbered with problems that they simply can't handle the hassle of long taxing waiting periods, and wrestling with the bureaucratic red tape, only to be denied by the Board of Veterans Appeal. For me, it has taken twenty-eight years of red tape. This long protracted struggle has produced unacceptable results for far too many of us.

Until the 1990s, a veteran seeking legal counsel had little or no chance of getting an attorney to represent his claim. This was because of the restriction by law that limits an attorney's fees to no more than $200.00, or the attorney would be subject to a $500.00 fine and/or two years in jail. It was the rare attorney indeed, who would agree to represent a veteran under such a stricture.

The 1990s did produce one change in the red tape, which was the establishment of a Court of Veterans Appeal. This resulted in another backlog of claims. This may help the process in the end but it leaves a lot to be desired in the all too long waiting process. Criminals are accorded a speedy trial, yet it takes heroes an eternity to get what has been justly earned by fulfilling their contractual obligations with sacrifice of life and limb.

The important things that any veteran should know are their entitlement by Congressional Law under Title 38 United States Code, Veterans Benefits. Although anyone can get the full copy from the Veterans Administration, on online, I have included crucial parts of that code for Veterans and their families to peruse:

CHAPTER 5 –
AUTHORITY AND DUTIES OF THE SECRETARY (pp. 42)
Subchapter
1 FORCE EDUCATION ASSISTANCE PROGRAM

SUBCHAPTER I – PURPOSES; DEFINITIONS

3001 Purposes
The purposes of this chapter are –

(1) To provide a new educational assistance program to assist in the readjustment of members of the Armed Forces to civilian life after their separation from military service.

(2) To extend the benefits of a higher education to qualifying men and women who might not otherwise be able to afford such an education.

(3) To provide for vocational readjustment and to restore lost educational opportunities to those service men and women who served active duty after June 30, 1985.

(4) To promote and assist the All-Volunteer Force program and the Total Force Concept of the Armed Forces by establishing a new program of educational assistance based upon service on active duty or a combination of service on active duty and in the Selected Reserve (including the National Guard) to aid in the recruitment and retention of highly qualified personnel for both the active and reserve components of the Armed Forces.

(5) To give special emphasis to providing educational assistance benefits to aid in the retention of personnel in the Armed Forces.

(6) To enhance our Nation's competitiveness through the development of a more highly educated and productive work force.

Besides knowing the benefits they are entitled to under Title 38 United States Code, Veterans Benefits, the Vietnam veterans ought to be keenly aware of and knowledgeable about, The Affirmative Action to Employ Disabled Veterans and Veterans of the Vietnam Era policies under 92-540 and 93-508 of the Vietnam Era Readjustment Act. There is no time for more acts of Congress and for studies that never end. There is no time for the bureaucratic red tape. Nothing short of emergency action can salvage those who have been deprived of those benefits that are already in place as mandated congressional laws. Proper implementation of 92-540 and 93-508 could still be beneficial in saving many of these vets as they get so close to the twilight of their lives.

I cite from my enormous file these brief accounts of my previous battles to drive home the point that the fight for Vietnam veterans benefits is a long and arduous one, full of red tape. No one in the groups of policy makers would collectively considered that morons might wage such a protracted struggle. These letters and transcripts, drawn from tons of paperwork, show the many roadblocks, delays, and resistance, which the Veterans' Administration put me through over the years. As I indicated earlier, many Vietnam veterans are too damaged physically and emotionally to face this long, frustrating challenge. They simply give up trying to get what is guaranteed to them by law.

Equipped with knowledge of his entitlements and rights, the Vietnam veteran still must throw himself into the fray with as much vigor as he put into the war. The following report from my medical files indicates the results of my willingness to fight back. On May 7, 1970, I received the following report from the United States Marine Corps. (Camp Pendleton, California):

> (1) The Secretary of the Navy has determined that you are physically unfit to perform the duties of your grade and has directed you be permanently retired by reason of physical disability under the provision of references (a) and (b). You are released from all active duty at 2400 on 18 May 1970 and transferred to the retired list of the Marine Corps/Marine Corps Reserve effective 19 May 1970. Your active duty pay accounts will be settled to include, 18 May 1970. Your pay entry based date is 17 November 1965. On 18 May 1970, you will have completed 4 years, 5 months and 19 days of active service

(2) Your disability is rated at 40 percent in accordance with the standard schedule for rating disabilities in current use by Veterans' Administration; VA Code(s) 5151, 5226

From that ruling, I went through numerous appeals fighting for a 100 percent disability rating. By April 4, 1982, a report from the Veterans' Administration read:

> A Rating Decision of this date increased the evaluation for residuals of head injury from 10 percent to 30 percent and granted service connection for tinnitus (10%) the combined evaluation is increased from 50 percent to 60 percent. Service connection for hearing loss, visual defect, gastro-intestinal disorder, skin disease, and residuals of "Agent Orange" exposure, and post-traumatic stress neurosis was denied.

On August 16, 1996, a letter from the Department of Veterans Affairs Office informed me of the following:

> I am writing to let you know that the regulations pertaining to service connection for herbicide exposure have been revised. This change may qualify Vietnam Era veterans for disability compensation....

Your name is listed on our Agent Orange Registry. We have identified you from this list as someone who might be eligible for service-connected compensation and health-care services from a condition we recognize as the result of exposure to herbicides used in the Vietnam.

On February 1, 1996, a letter to me from the Department of Veterans Affairs read in parts:

We have granted your claim for service-connected disability compensation for the following Condition Percentage Post-traumatic stress disorder 50% combined evaluation: 80%. We denied your claim for increased services-connected disability compensation for traumatic encephalopathy with manifestations of headache, dizziness, and mild ocular imbalance currently evaluated at 30%. We denied your claim for service-connection for visual loss as new and material evidence has not been submitted to reopen your claim.

On August 12, 1996, I received the following letter from the Department of Veterans Affairs, which reads in part:

> We have granted your claim for increased service-connected disability compensation based on individual unemployability.

Issue:
Entitlement to individual unemployability
Evidence:
See Dating of 1-20-96
Decision:
Entitlement to individual unemployability is granted effective October 17, 1995
Reason and Basis:
The veteran indicated that his physical and emotional problems are such that he can neither work nor attend school. He has last worked full-time in 1994. This is entirely consistent with the evidence of record including the recent increase in the veteran's PTSD symptoms. Entitlement to individual unemployability is granted because the claimant is unable to secure or follow a substantially gainful occupation as a result of service-connected disabilities. Reasonable doubt has been resolved in favor of claimant.

When reading just these few notes from my account, you

may note that the military and the Veterans Administration never do pull the records of the initial injuries. You may also note how long it takes them to refer back to the initial detailing of injuries received in the beginning; this enforces my point that they don't consider my injuries and the connected problems to be service related.

This is, of course patently absurd, since I clearly did not expose myself to Agent Orange or embed shrapnel in my own body. It is apparent that the powers-that-be failed to consider all of my wounds and their effects properly. I feel that these avoidances were intentional on their part. I believe this avoidance has been successfully done to shirk their responsibility to assist those who without the wherewithal and intelligence to hang in there for the course, and take the beating of running the gauntlet. Had I not realized the depth of the problems facing those unfortunate comrades, I probably would not have mustered the fortitude necessary to make it to this point, and I remain at a loss of how this has came to be in my case. I do know that those who can't fight, for whatever reasons, have fueled my passion to do whatever I can to make things better.

I make no claim to have suffered personally in exactly the same ways that all veterans have collectively suffered, but I do know about the violations of the Vietnam Era Readjustment Act of 1972. One of the most important parts of rehabilitating the veterans after arriving stateside was employment. It was to give Vietnam veterans preference over non-veteran applicants in federally mandated affirmative action programs. I do know firsthand about the devastating effects of post-traumatic stress disorder and failures of the system to address the treatment of this psychological and emotional injury properly. I do know of the multiple chemical agents, other than Agent Orange, which have been scarcely publicized or talked about, but which have effects nevertheless as deadly. I do know of the horrendous effects these chemicals have had in contributing to the sickness and death of Vietnam veterans. I do know of the difficulties of the veterans in getting medical treatment and disability benefits, which law entitles to them. I do know of the absolute belligerence on the part of the government administration that still intentionally neglects and totally violates congressional laws. In other words, through my personal Vietnam and post-Vietnam experiences, through my activism on behalf of Vietnam veterans, and through my own success in winning my own rights to full benefits, I am starkly aware that I have enough in common with my fellow veterans to speak on their behalf. I have the knowledge and empathy to tell them what they must do to get help, receive their just due benefits, and become empowered.

The Affirmative Action benefits from the Department of Labor, public law 92-540 and 93-508, were enacted so that government contractors would give preference for employment to disabled and Vietnam era veterans. Those provisions are as follows:

> What it is:
> "Affirmative action" is the legal obligation of every employer doing business with the Federal Government under a contract or subcontract of $10,000 or more to employ and advance in employment, disabled veterans of all wars, and all veterans of the Vietnam Era.

This legal obligation calls for the contractor not to discriminate against any employee or applicant for employment because he or she is a disabled veteran or a veteran of the Vietnam Era. It also calls for the contractor to treat qualified veterans without discrimination because of their disability or their veterans' status.

Why?

Certainly, over the years, American business and industry have hired disabled veterans and veterans of the Vietnam Era. Yet far too many veterans have not had an equal opportunity to work, or to get ahead in their jobs. The purpose of affirmative action is to assure that qualified veterans get this equal opportunity. By requiring government contractors and subcontractors to comply with the law, affirmative action should result in more qualified disabled veterans and veterans of the Vietnam Era entering the labor force. In addition, affirmative action should lead to greater participation by more employers in the hiring of veterans.

The Legal Basis:

December 3, 1974: was the birth of Public Law 93-508, the Vietnam Era Veterans' Readjustment Act of 1974. The law amended the Vietnam Era Veterans' Readjustment Assistance Act of 1972 (Public Law 92-540). One of the notable changes was the replacement of the words "special emphasis" with the words "affirmative action" regarding the employment of veterans. This was the legal basis, the beginning of affirmative action.

The Office of Federal Contract Compliance Programs of the US Department of Labor on June 25, 1976, issued regulations on "Affirmative Action Obligations of Contractors and Subcontractors for disabled Veterans and Veterans of the Vietnam Era." They dealt specifically with Section 402 of the law.

How Many Contractors?

About half of all the businesses in America some 3,000,000 are covered by Section 402. Therefore, a majority of the industrial leaders of the United States are responsible for some form of affirmative action.

Who is a Disabled Veteran?

A disabled veteran is a person who:

    1. Is entitled to disability compensation under laws administered by the Veterans Administration for disability, rated at 30 percent or more; or,

    2. Was discharged or released from active duty due to a disability incurred or aggravated in the line of duty.

(Veterans with non-service-connected disabilities aren't eligible under this law, but may be under section 503 of the Rehabilitation Act.)

Who is a Veteran of the Vietnam Era?

A veteran of the Vietnam Era is a person who:

    1. Served on active duty for a period of more than 180 days, any part of which occurred between August 5, 1964 and May 7, 1975 and was discharged or released from that duty with a discharge other than dishonorable; or

    2. Was discharged or released from active duty for a service-connected disability if any part of such duty was performed between August 5, 1964 and May 7, 1975.

    Also, the veteran must have been discharged or released within forty-eight months preceding the alleged affirmative action violation.

Is Every Disabled and Vietnam Era Veteran Covered?

No. As well as being a "disabled veteran" or a "veteran of the Vietnam Era," the veteran also must be "qualified" for the job. That is, the veteran must be capable of performing a particular job, with in the case of the disabled veteran reasonable accommodation to his or her disability.

How Many Disabled Veterans?

Of the 29.5 million American veterans in the US, there were 2,300,000 active compensation cases in mid-1976, according to the Veterans Administration. Included were disabled veterans of World War II, and the Korean conflict, as well as those of the Vietnam Era (World War II: 1,700,000; Korean conflict; 154,000).

How Many Veterans of the Vietnam Era?

Veterans Administration statistics show there were some 8 million veterans who served during the Vietnam Era. (Of this figure, 458,000 were active compensation cases; that is, disabled veterans.)

How Many Disabled Veterans and Veterans of the Vietnam Era are Covered by Section 402?

Applying the definitions of "eligible" disabled and Vietnam Era veterans, there are about 1 million disabled veterans and 7.9 million Vietnam Era veterans or a total of 8.9 million veterans who could be thought of as a target population for affirmative action.

Obviously, a large percentage of these nearly 9 million veterans are employed, while a small percent are "unemployable" due to the nature of their disability. However, as of the middle of 1976, nearly 600,000 veterans were unemployed and this figure was only for Vietnam Era veterans between the ages of 20 and 34 (These figures from the Bureau of Labor Statistics).

By an estimate, the number of disabled and Vietnam Era veterans not employed, or not getting ahead in employment, is far too high. It is the aim of affirmative action to reduce these numbers.

What Government Contracts Are Included?

Included are contracts of $10,000 or more for the furnishing of supplies or services, or for the use of real or personal property, including lease arrangements and construction. Sub-contracts are also included. The word "services" includes utility, transportation, research, insurance, and fund depository. "Construction" means the construction, rehabilitation, alteration, conversion, extension, demolition, or repair of buildings, highways or other changes or improvements to real property. Also included are the supervision, inspection, and other onsite functions involved in the actual construction.

Agreements in which the parties stand in the relationship of employer and employee and federally assisted contracts are not considered "Government Contracts" for affirmative action. Work outside the United States, contracts, and subcontracts for indefinite quantities are not included. There are a few other exceptions.

Affirmative Action Clauses

Each agency and each contractor and subcontractor must include an affirmative action clause in each of its covered Government contracts or subcontracts. The clause must cover the following points, among others:

1. The contractor will not discriminate against any qualified employee or applicant for employment because he or she is a disabled veteran or Vietnam Era veteran. The contractor also agrees to take affirmative action to employ, advance in employment, and treat without discrimination disabled veterans and veterans of the Vietnam Era.

2. The contractor agrees that all suitable employment openings of the contractor will be listed at the appropriate local office of the state employment service system, and to provide such

reports regarding openings and hirings as may be required.

3. The contractor shall advise the employment service system, in each state where it has establishments if the name and location of each hiring location in the state.

4. The contractor agrees to comply with the rules, regulations, and orders the Secretary of Labor issued in accordance with P.L. 93-508.

5. In the event of non-compliance, actions may be taken according to the rules, regulations, and orders of the Secretary of Labor

6. The contractor agrees to post in conspicuous places, available to employees and applications for employment, notices stating affirmative action obligations under law.

7. The contractor will notify each labor union or worker representative that he (the contractor) is bound by P.L. 93-508, and is committed to take affirmative action to employ and advance in employment qualified disabled and Vietnam Era veterans.

8. The contractor will include the affirmative action clause in every subcontractor or purchase order of $10,000 or more, unless exempted, so that the clause will be binding on each subcontractor or vender. He will take such action to enforce the clause for subcontracts and purchase orders as directed.

For Larger Contractors:

Within 120 days of the beginning of the contract, every government contractor or subcontractor holding a contract of $50,000 or more and having 50 or more employees must prepare and maintain an affirmative action program which sets forth his policies, practices, and procedures regarding disabled and Vietnam Era veteran employees.

This program may be integrated into, or kept separate from other affirmative action programs of the contractor, but contractors presently holding government contracts must update their affirmative action programs within 120 days of July 26, 1976.

The affirmative action program must be reviewed and updated each year. Any significant changes in the rights or benefits must be communicated to employees and applicants for employment. The full affirmative action program must be available for inspection to any employee or applicant for employment upon request, and the location and hours during which the program may be obtained must be posted at each facility.

The sad fact is that this law and these policies were enacted nearly forty years ago, and are still not adhered to. Vietnam Era veterans and disabled veterans in general still have difficulties finding gainful employment, in spite of their great service to our country.

Chapter 11

THINGS THAT HAPPENED BEFORE AND CONTINUE TODAY

Many people in this country don't know all there is to know about the crisis caused by the Vietnam War's effects. We have a tendency to feel as though the ramifications are resolved. This thinking is dangerous because the hazards are repeating themselves and ever evolving today.

A factor that has been put aside in the Vietnam veteran's community is now showing up in a tremendous way among veterans of the Iraq and Afghanistan wars. The occurrence of brain trauma caused by IED's or Improvised Explosive Devices is well documented to be prevalent in veterans of Iraq and Afghanistan, and the world is now aware of the damages to the brain caused by immediate proximity to these explosives. The US government speaks of these brain injuries as a 'new phenomena,' but these injuries happened quite often to Vietnam veterans and were not recognized as debilitating injuries by the Veteran's Administration or the Social Security Administration. To this day, I personally suffer from brain injuries acquired from immediate proximity to explosives such as mortars, rockets, artillery rounds, and booby traps. In the early years of claiming these disorders, however, the Veterans Administration denied that these injuries really existed, regardless of the symptoms.

Today, there are Vietnam veterans who are still being denied disability compensation, as if the close proximity blasts of the Vietnam War era were less disabling than the IEDs of today.

How can it take so long to realize this, with so many cases having been claimed for so long; and how many veterans of today will have to endure the same fate as the Vietnam veterans? We are still experiencing veterans returning from the Iraq and from Afghanistan having difficulty with claims and becoming street dwellers, living in cars, and under freeway ramps, and not receiving proper care. It is very important to keep the past ever present, or we are doomed to repeat it.

In Vietnam, it was Agent Orange. In Iraq, it is depleted Uranium. Some are still having problems with Gulf War syndrome from Desert Storm and the problems are almost guaranteed to carry on.

It also seems that we are rapidly heading to the next instituted draft. Right now, people who have committed crimes are being accepted into military service as an alternative to jail time. Many disadvantaged youth are recruited directly from high school, with recruiters a daily presence, using high-pressure sales tactics to swell the ranks of our fighting force. These children are told that the military is their only path to a better life and the American Dream. Today's military still maintains the right to accept lower mental standards in recruitment, thus the same socially under-privileged, poor, uneducated, and mentally challenged, with a low tenth to fifth percentile test score can be enlisted when necessary. It very well can be argued that the tenth percentile grade on the military standards tests are indications of how low the Defense Department would go to achieve bodies for the war effort. In Vietnam, there were numerous people accepted who should have been rejected due to physical problems. It is more than conceivable that the mental standards were less than the tenth percentile range.

I witnessed trainees who couldn't read adequately to understand their basic handbook. With the IQ standard stating that less than 70 IQ was considered retarded, it's rather apparent that there were a percentage of retarded people accepted to active duty by the Defense Department.

The military then began to give GED testing to draftees during 1968. But many of these tests were conducted in Vietnam, without preparatory classes and under duress. I was included in the GED testing shortly after being wounded. Many of the Project 100,000 troops took the test without preparatory classes; it didn't do them any good. By the time GED testing was available for "new standard troops," many had been killed or wounded. They were then discharged without any knowledge of the proposed benefits. Even if they did know, what would these resources be, since Congress never approved the proposal?

It is now apparent that the US and her allies have embarked on the fight against terrorism throughout the world. It is also apparent that our military is over-extended, thereby increasing the potential for enacting the draft. With this appearing to be imminent, we must guard against repeating the horrors of forcing the less privileged social groups to fight the fight and therefore possibly to suffer the same atrocities that have, and still are, affecting our veterans since the Vietnam Era.

Chapter 12

A FINAL WORD
TO VIETNAM VETERANS

Some of us were recruited for the "police action" in Vietnam under special circumstances. Those circumstances amounted to getting America's poorest citizens to fight an unpopular war on behalf of the rich and the powerful. Some of us were ridiculed and laughed at. The standard joke was that we were members of "The Moron Corps." But if my story has demonstrated nothing else, I hope that it has shown that in combat, there are no morons. There is no distinction between Project 100,000 recruits and anybody else. Under fire, the Viet Cong knew no distinctions. They were trying to kill Americans, regardless of race, class, status, or IQ scores. Therefore, it appears to me that no matter how lesser a person is considered to be, patriotism should be judged by their sacrifices, and their efforts to contribute to their country and government.

As it turned out, it was not until Vietnam veterans returned home in general that we were really treated like morons. After returning home, our government wanted to sweep us aside and relegate us to the dustbin of history. More significantly, it wanted to deny us our just claims for the rights, entitlements, and benefits due to us.

As a student of history, I have witnessed our government

enacting "Marshall Plans," foreign aid, and other costly schemes to rebuild countries that we had previously declared to be our enemies countries whose leaders were responsible for the deaths of thousands of Americans. I have also witnessed cases where the government has misused people in the past, without being aware of the violations and coming through late with necessary actions to correct the problem.

I would suggest that our government step up and do what is right, by taking action for these veterans who have been used, mistreated, humiliated, and denied their rights. The government owes them more than can ever be repaid. After all, much has been done for lesser heroes or deserving people. Instead, our government has a way of pardoning the guys who did the crime and sentencing us to do the time.

I am particularly dismayed that in Congress, in both the House and the Senate, and in lesser political offices all over America, Vietnam veterans in positions of power have shown the same lack of enthusiasm to help their fellow Vietnam veterans. I ask: Are your political aspirations more important than we, your comrades, are? When will you stop to help the comrades who need you? How far will you go? You were there and should know the hell we went through in correcting the injustice. You should be leading the fight for action on behalf of your Vietnam War comrades!

We cannot wait on the government to seek us out and find us. The ineffectual outreach programs that have been proposed over the years have failed miserably. The authorities have failed to reach those veterans who are outside of the routine bureaucratic flow, such as those living in rural areas similar to those communities that I come from. Some basic, vital information has only reached certain less privileged veterans by word-of-mouth. When a few finally get information, it is often less than informative and effective in the purpose of bringing them in for help with their numerous problems. In effect, it appears to these veterans as more of the same to which they've become accustomed, thus continuing the trend of frustration and neglect.

These isolated communities spawn despair, and hopelessness for those lost to the system. These veterans are the fruit of all races of those communities: Blacks, Hispanics, Asians, Indians, and poor Whites. Those of us who survive, look upon government programs as another "Hook and Crook" in the running of the gauntlet. The war goes on.

Thus, it is not only necessary for the Vietnam veteran to take the initiative in finding out what his or her rights and entitlements are, it is imperative. Remember, no fight, no win!

I want to leave a final word to my fellow veterans regarding steps they might take to get the ball rolling on their behalf. Even as I write these words, the medical effects of my Vietnam wounds and particularly my exposure to Agent Orange and other chemicals used in the war are steadily taking away my life. However, I am not in despair. I am not depressed. I am a warrior. Therefore, I am still fighting back. No fight, no win.

The first thing I want to leave with veterans, and anyone interested in their plight, is that the key to demanding what veterans of any war rightfully deserve is to have a thorough knowledge about Veterans Administration benefits.

Knowing some of these benefits will tend to raise their confidence level and maybe their incentive to seek treatment and adjudication of their claims. I would suggest that the veteran seeking help first know the following rules of veteran's benefits:

1.   Any veterans having served in the active military of the United State during a war campaign or expedition, having served ninety days or more in the combat area who alleges any disease or injury as being service-connected, even with no record of

this disease or injury shall be given the benefit of doubt as to his or her claim, unless otherwise proven by the government. Numerous Army veterans have complained about the Army and Veterans Administrations failing to proceed with their claims, blaming such things as the fire at the St. Louis record centers as the reason for not being able to come to a favorable decision on behalf of the veteran. This I have proven to be against these veterans' claims when it really shouldn't.

2. The Secretary of Veterans Affairs determined that benefits administered by the department were not provided due to administrative error on the part of the Federal Government or any of its employees. The Secretary may provide such relief because of such error as is determined equitable; including the payment of moneys to whoever is deserving. Knowing this, the veteran is at least aware that he or she does not have to accept any decision by the Veterans Administration or be caught up in red tape and bogus denials.

3. It has been said that if you don't know, you don't get. My experience has proven this to be true in practically every situation regarding veteran's benefits. So educate yourself, be fearless about asking questions, demand answers. Knowledge is power.

4. The veterans should choose the best-qualified representatives to fight for them. However, this could be difficult, so I would strongly suggest the veteran join the Disabled American Veterans for the best available representation, since they have a proven track record of being sincere and aggressive in fighting on behalf of veterans with a stick-to-it attitude.

5. If possible, the veteran should make a list of all problems experienced during and since the war, since this will better enable the doctors to correlate known problems and associate these with disease and injuries. This is true especially for Post Traumatic Stress Disorder, which plagues many veterans.

6.   Help those who cannot help themselves. This is needed more so than anything. For without our help, many veterans will remain lost and unaware of what to do.

7.   Those who can, should read all they can about Title 38 US Code Veteran Benefits and stay with it. There is hope.

8.   Vietnam veterans should know that rarely is there a decision made in favor of the veteran at the regional level. This is the level where so many veterans quit, rather than appeal to the Board of Veterans Appeals. Even if unsuccessful at the Board of Veterans Appeals level, the veteran should appeal to the Court of Veterans Appeals. In other words, this fight for our rights sometimes requires us to compete with the red tape up to the highest levels of appeal, if necessary. While this might tend to wear on one's patience, hang in there. No fight, no win.

9.   Veterans need to know that when most Vietnam veterans were filing service-connected disabilities, there was not a Court of Veterans Appeals. Now that the court is established, cases can be reopened on disabilities that were previously denied. Post Traumatic Stress Disorder has been handled with more consideration through the court and all of the roadblocks have been opened for those who seek treatment and disability claims.

It is also due to the decision of the court that every claim has to run the entire bureaucratic gauntlet and can now be adjudicated at the regional level. Therefore, the veteran should make the Court of Veterans Appeals one of the chief weapons in his fight.

Personally, I have won many of my battles for benefits, even though the process has been arduous and frustrating. I now spend my time fighting for the rights of other veterans, particularly those who were referred to as morons. I speak to all those who want to hear about the War in Vietnam and its aftermath. In between time, I get the chance to get in a little hunting, fishing, and gardening. I try to enjoy some of those things I used to enjoy as a boy, growing up in Missouri. I wrote this book over a period of years. It had been written indelibly on my mind before it was actually put to paper. Although reliving the events was painful, it also turned out to be therapeutic.

I wrote not just to tell my story, but also, I hope to inspire other Vietnam veterans in a similar predicament or worse, to be encouraged with knowledge about the benefits they rightly deserve. Please hang in there, fight back, and don't give into the drugs, alcohol, suicide, homelessness, prison, and all of the daily fires that consume us in civilian life. If my account can inspire one Vietnam veteran to adopt the attitude or motto of "no fight, no win," then it would have been worth it. No fight, no win. This was true in Vietnam when politicians stopped us from fighting the war to win by simply bombing the Viet Cong into oblivion. The no fight no win policy applies even more to our lives after Vietnam, because for so many of us the war goes on still.

I am actually glad that I have a so-called narcissistic personality that gives me "a very high regard" for myself and for my future. I do feel that the Vietnam veteran is a victim. I feel this is not just perceived but real; and if I pursue my rights and those of other veterans in a "narrow and rigid way," then so be it. The problem that so many of us veterans face is the inability to focus our emotions, to channel so much rage, anger, and hurt into something positive something that will be beneficial to our friends, families, and our communities. I believe the Vietnam veteran owes it to himself to make his greatest cause himself, and to make it his lifetime work to be strong again. Once strong again, he can make a stand on his own behalf and on behalf of his Vietnam comrades

✪ ✪ ✪

Printed in the USA
CPSIA information can be obtained
at www.ICGtesting.com
CBHW031307121223
2582CB00005BA/298